TOVE FEVANG

CROCHET
for the
KITCHEN

TRAFALGAR SQUARE
North Pomfret, Vermont

First published in the United States of America in 2013 by

Trafalgar Square Books
North Pomfret, Vermont 05053
www.trafalgarbooks.com

Originally published in Norway in 2012 as *Hekling & Hakking til Kjøkkenet* by Cappelen Damm AS

© 2012 Cappelen Damm AS
English translation © 2013 Trafalgar Square Books

ISBN: 978-1-57076-606-0

Library of Congress Control Number:
2012952547

Translation: Carol Huebscher Rhoades
Photography: Ragnar Hartvig
Detail Photos: Geir Arnesen
Stylist: Ingrid Skansaar
Book design: Laila Gundersen

Printed in China

10 9 8 7 6 5 4 3 2 1

Table of Contents

Foreword

My work with various magazines and yarn manufacturers inspired this book. Åse Myrvold Egeland, at the magazine *Family*, often asked if I had some potholders they could use.

I began to think about all those old potholders I remembered from my childhood. There were potholders with ruffles on a filet crochet base, dresses and jackets. Some even had a plastic base surrounded by crochet.

When I first asked family and friends if they had any old potholders, many of the same patterns popped up but in every possible color and shape. Like many other types of handwork, potholder designs have been passed from household to household but with only verbal rather than written instructions. Most of the crochet patterns from long ago had a more oral tradition than today. Everyone clearly knew what a mousetooth edging was. Earlier patterns would just say, "crochet mouse-teeth around the edge," (*Women and Clothing*, no 7, 1940). The pattern is what we now call a picot edging, with a detailed description specifying how many chain stitches are needed before joining them with a single crochet.

Potholders are something we all need, and they can be worked in regular or Tunisian crochet. The items are hardly bigger than a swatch so, in a short amount of time, you can make one. Experiment with different yarns, color combinations or new stitches. It's also a great way to learn how to crochet, at the same time you'll have made something useful. Make some for yourself or give them away as presents.

If you haven't done regular or Tunisian crochet before, you'll find a "Crochet School" at the back of this books starting on page 110. One of the exciting aspects of crochet is that there are so many possible structures that can be combined. Nothing is absolutely right or crazy. So, make color changes, use different yarns and techniques, and make it your own.

I have had a lot of excellent help with the projects in this book. My husband, Geir Arnesen, who has, yet again, taken the step-by-step photos at all hours, is a patient photographer who brings much more than just photo angles to the process. Berit Østlie helped me with some of the projects when time was short. Ingrid Skaansar and Ragnar Hartvig styled and photographed all of the lovely background settings for the designs in this book. Last, but not least, thanks to my publisher's editor, Inger-Margrethe Karlsen, who also had faith in this project and made it possible to complete. Many thanks to everyone – without each and every one of you, this book would not have been possible.

If you have a crochet hook and a ball of yarn, you have everything you need to start a new potholder or placemat.

Good luck!

Best wishes, Tove

www.tovefevang.no

Introduction

CROCHET TOOLS

To crochet, all you need is a hook the size appropriate for the yarn. Scissors and needles are also necessary for finishing and weaving in ends.

Crochet hooks are available in an assortment of materials: metal, plastic, bamboo, and wood. Wood hooks are my favorite are because they fit well in my hand and are very comfortable to use. If you buy a crochet hook set with sizes U.S. D-3 – J-10 / 3 – 10 mm, you'll always have the right size on hand and you can easily find the one needed to suit your yarn and gauge.

BEGINNING OR ENDING A PIECE

Many patterns tell you to chain loosely. It's not always easy to do that and it's a good rule of thumb to use a larger size hook than that specified for the piece. For example, if the instructions say to use an H-8 / 5 mm hook, then working the beginning chain with a J-9 / 5.5 mm hook will provide an edge that doesn't pull in, an important factor for the look of the finished piece.

And when finishing, work the final or last two rows or rounds with one U.S. size or one-half metric size smaller hook. Sometimes crochet work draws in a bit but you don't want that to happen on the last rows/rounds. If you worked the piece with an H-8 / 5 mm hook, then finishing with a US 7 / 4.5 mm will insure that the edge will not be looser than the piece as a whole.

Tip! When you begin a piece with a lot of chain stitches, it's not always easy to keep count of the number of chains. To insure that you have enough chains, make a few extra. You can undo any extra chains after you've worked the first row. Make sure that the knot at the beginning of the chain is not too tight. When there are extra chain sts, unpick the knot and then use a hook to undo the extra chain stitches. When you are even with the end of the first row, pull the yarn tail through firmly.

CROCHETING IN ROWS

When you get to the end of the first row across, turn the work. You can turn clockwise or counterclockwise. Decide how you want to turn and then work the same way throughout the piece. At the beginning of the next row, make the correct number of chain stitches (ch) to substitute for the first st (sc, dc, hdc, dc, tr, etc). Make 1 ch for a sc, 2 for a hdc, 3 for a dc, 4 for tr, and 5 for dbl tr.

CROCHETING IN THE ROUND

Instead of crocheting back and forth in rows, you can work in the round. Begin with the number of chain stitches specified in the instructions and then join the ring with a slip stitch into the first chain loop. If you are going to make a flat disk, make sure that the increases are evenly spaced around throughout. If you are making a tube, crochet around and around without increasing. Each round begins with the same number of chain sts appropriate for the stitch (see Crocheting in Rows). End each round with a slip st into the first st of the round.

DIFFERENTIATING ROWS AND ROUNDS IN A PATTERN

When you crochet back and forth, you are working in rows. When you crochet around, you are working in rounds.

Once you know if a piece is worked in rows or rounds, then you will understand how the piece is constructed. Sometimes both methods are used in one piece. For example, you might be crocheting netting for a bag in the round but then you crochet the handles back and forth.

JOINING YARN AND CHANGING COLORS

It is best to change or join yarn at the side of a piece or at the beginning of a round but sometimes that isn't possible. In that case, catch one yarn tail with the stitches as you crochet and catch the other yarn end on the next round or row. Tails can also be woven in during finishing by threading into the backs of stitches with a tapestry needle.

Usually colors are changed at the beginning of a round or at the side. For a smooth transition between the colors, work as follows: before you begin the last stitch prior to the color change, make sure that the yarn to be dropped is on the wrong side of the piece. Crochet to the last yarnover on the stitch with the old color, yarn over hook with the new color and pull new color through on the last step of the stitch. Now continue with the new color. In this way, each of the stitches will each be worked in its own color.

CROCHET GAUGE

Each pattern specifies the gauge and you should make a swatch to test the gauge. Crochet a swatch about 6 x 6 in / 15 x 15 cm and take measurements within the center 4 x 4 in / 10 x 10 cm. Count the number of stitches and rows. It is important to make a gauge swatch bigger than 4 x 4 in / 10 x 10 cm because it will pull in a bit at the outer edges. If the stitch count doesn't match that in the pattern, change to a larger or smaller size hook. If there are too many stitches,

change to a larger hook and, if there are too few stitches, use a smaller hook.

Tunisian Crochet

Tunisian crochet has several alternate names, such as Tunisian knitting or Afghan crochet. In this book, we'll use the term Tunisian crochet as it is the most common.

The technique produces one of the sturdiest fabrics you can make so it is good for both placemats and potholders. The stitches won't unravel; each row consists of a forward and a return pass so each stitch is locked in. In order to work Tunisian crochet, you need a special Tunisian crochet hook. These hooks are long, straight, and even all down the shaft so you won't have any depression for holding onto the hook. The Tunisian crochet hook has to be long, with a stopper at one end so that there is enough room to hold all the stitches from a row without any falling off. Some Tunisian crochet hooks have a hook at each end so that you can work in the round. All of the Tunisian crochet projects in this book use a hook with a hook at only one end.

All Tunisian crochet projects begin with a chain stitch foundation that you can work with a regular crochet hook one size smaller than the Tunisian hook you'll use to prevent the stitches from being too loose in relation to the Tunisian crochet.

Tunisian Crochet Tools

For Tunisian crochet, all you need is a Tunisian crochet hook the size appropriate for the yarn. Scissors and needles are also used for finishing and weaving in ends. Crochet hooks are available in an assortment of materials: metal, plastic, bamboo, and wood. Wood hooks are my favorite are because they fit well in my hand and are very comfortable to use.

As for regular crochet, you can buy a set of Tunisian crochet hooks in a range of sizes. It is also good to have a regular crochet hook for chaining the stitches at the beginning of a piece and for finishing.

Tip! When you begin a piece with a lot of chain stitches, it's not always easy to keep count of the number of chains. To insure that you have enough chains, make a few extra. You can undo any extra chains after you've worked the first row. Make sure that the knot at the beginning of the chain is not too tight. When there are extra chain sts, unpick the knot and then use a hook to undo the extra chain stitches. When you are even with the end of the first row, pull the yarn tail through firmly.

TUNISIAN CROCHET ROWS

All of the completed rows in Tunisian crochet consist of two steps: a forward row and a return row.

TUNISIAN CROCHET GAUGE

Each pattern specifies the gauge and you should make a swatch to test the gauge. Crochet a swatch about 6 x 6 in / 15 x 15 cm and take measurements within the center 4 x 4 in / 10 x 10 cm. Count the number of stitches and rows. It is important to make a gauge swatch bigger than 4 x 4 in / 10 x 10 cm because it will pull in a bit at the outer edges. If the stitch count doesn't match that in the pattern, change to a larger or smaller size hook. If there are too many stitches, change to a larger hook and, if there are too few stitches, use a smaller hook.

BUY ENOUGH YARN

It is important to have enough yarn on hand before you start a piece. If you've already begun and have to buy more yarn, you may not be able to get the same dyelot and the colors won't match.

I also recommended that you always use good quality yarn to ensure the best results and the most enjoyable crocheting. The process is as important as the finished result!

Natural Delight

Striped Potholder with Small Bobbles

MEASUREMENTS:	Approx. 8 x 8 in / 20 x 20 cm
MATERIALS:	CYCA #2, PT All Year (100% cotton; 87 yd/80 m / 50 g) / Natural 219, 50 g / Beige 220, 50 g
CROCHET HOOK:	U.S. size G-6 / 4 mm for potholder and U.S. F-5 / 3.75 mm for edging
GAUGE:	21 sts in pattern with larger hook = 4 in / 10 cm

Instructions:

With larger hook and Natural, ch 35.

Row 1: Work 2 dc in 2nd ch from hook, skip 2 ch, *1 sc, 2 dc in next ch, skip 2 ch*; rep from * to * and end with 1 sc in the last ch; turn.

Row 2: Ch 1, 2 dc in sc, skip 2 dc, *1 sc, 2 dc in next sc, skip 2 dc*; rep from * to * and end with 1 sc in ch from previous row; turn.

Row 3: Change to Beige. Work 2 dc in sc, skip 2 dc, *in next sc, work 1 sc and 2 dc, skip 2 dc; * rep from * to * and end with 1 sc in last ch; turn.

Row 4: Ch 1, 2 dc in sc, skip 2 dc, *in next sc, work 1 sc and 2 dc, skip 2 dc*; rep from * to * and end with 1 sc in ch from previous row; turn.

Row 5: Change to Natural. Work 2 dc in sc, skip 2 dc, *work 1 sc and 2 dc in next sc, skip 2 dc*; rep from * to * across and end with 1 sc in last ch; turn.

Row 6: Ch 1, 2 dc in sc, skip 2 dc, *1 sc, 2 dc in next sc, skip 2 dc*; rep from * to * and end with 1 sc in ch from previous row; turn.

Repeat Rows 3 – 6: 6 times.

EDGING:

Rnd 1: Change to smaller hook and Beige. Attach yarn with 1 sl st in corner st, work 3 sc in corner st, 1 sc in each st, 3 sc in corner st.
2nd side: Work 1 sc in each row and 3 sc in corner st.
3rd side: Work 1 sc in each ch (= foundation chain), 3 sc in corner st.
4th side: Work 1 sc in each row and end with 1 sl st into 1st sc.

Rnd 2: Work 1 sc in each sc; in each corner st, work 3 sc; end with 1 sl st into 1st sc.

Rnd 3: Change to Natural. Work 1 sl st in each sc around, ending 1 sc before last corner. Make a hanging loop in the last corner: Ch 10, skip corner (= 3 sc) and skip next sc; attach loop into next sl st with 1 sl st. Cut yarn and fasten off.

FINISHING: Weave in all ends neatly on WS and gently steam press potholder.

Make another potholder the same way.

Potholder
with Small Bobbles

MEASUREMENTS:	Approx. 8 x 8 in / 20 x 20 cm
MATERIALS:	CYCA # 2, PT All Year (100% cotton; 87 yd/80 m / 50 g) / Natural 219, 100 g / Beige 220, 50 g
CROCHET HOOK:	U.S. size G-6 / 4 mm for potholder and U.S. F-5 / 3.75 mm for edging
GAUGE:	21 sts in pattern with larger hook = 4 in / 10 cm

Instructions:

With larger hook and Natural, ch 35.

Row 1: Work 2 dc in 2nd ch from hook, skip 2 dc, *1 sc, 2 dc in next ch, skip 2 ch*; rep from * to * and end with 1 sc in the last ch; turn.

Row 2: Ch 1, 2 dc in sc, skip 2 dc, *1 sc, 2 dc in next sc, skip 2 dc*; rep from * to * and end with 1 sc in ch from previous row; turn.

Rows 3 – 26: Rep Row 2 (or work until potholder is square).

EDGING:

Rnd 1: Change to smaller hook and Beige. Attach yarn with 1 sl st in corner, work 3 sc in corner st, 1 sc in each st, 3 sc in corner st. Next side: Work 1 sc in each row and 3 sc in corner st. Next side: Work 1 sc in each ch (= foundation chain), 3 sc in corner st. Last side: Work 1 sc in each row and end with 1 sl st into 1st sc.

Rnd 2: Work 1 sc in each sc; in each corner, work 3 sc; end with 1 sl st into 1st sc.

Rnd 3: Work 1 sl st in each sc around, ending 1 sc before last corner. Make a hanging loop in the last corner: Ch 10, skip corner (= 3 sc) and skip next sc; attach loop into next sl st with 1 sl st. Cut yarn and fasten off.

FINISHING: Weave in all ends neatly on WS and gently steam press potholder.

Make another potholder the same way.

Single Crochet
Potholder

MEASUREMENTS:	Approx. 8 x 8 in / 20 x 20 cm
MATERIALS:	CYCA # 2, PT All Year (100% cotton; 87 yd/80 m / 50 g) / White 296, 50 g / Beige 220, 100 g
CROCHET HOOK:	U.S. size G-6 / 4 mm for potholder and U.S. F-5 / 3.75 mm for edging
GAUGE:	19 sc in pattern with larger hook = 4 in / 10 cm

Instructions:

With larger hook and Beige, ch 34.

Row 1: Work 1 sc in 2nd ch from hook, work 1 sc in every ch across = 33 sts; turn.
Row 2: Ch 1, 1 sc in back loop of each sc across = 33 sts; turn.
Rows 3 – 38: Ch 1, 1 sc in back loop of each sc across = 33 sts; turn.

EDGING:
Rnd 1: Change to smaller hook and White. Attach yarn with 1 sl st in corner, work 3 sc in corner st, 1 sc in each st, 3 sc in corner st.

2nd side: Work 1 sc in each row (make sure the edge doesn't ruffle or pucker) and 3 sc in corner st.
3rd side: Work 1 sc in each ch (= foundation chain), 3 sc in corner st.
4th side: Work 1 sc in each row and end with 1 sl st into 1st sc.
Rnd 2: Work 1 sl st in each sc around, ending 1 sc before last corner. Make a hanging loop in the last corner: Ch 10, skip corner (= 3 sc) and skip next sc; attach loop into next sl st with 1 sl st. Cut yarn and fasten off.

FINISHING: Weave in all ends neatly on WS and gently steam press potholder.

Make another potholder the same way.

Striped Single Crochet Potholder

MEASUREMENTS:	Approx. 8 x 8 in / 20 x 20 cm
MATERIALS:	CYCA #2, PT All Year (100% cotton; 87 yd/80 m / 50 g) / White 296, 100 g / Beige 220, 50 g
CROCHET HOOK:	U.S. size G-6 / 4 mm for potholder and U.S. F-5 / 3.75 mm for edging
GAUGE:	19 sc in pattern with larger hook = 4 in / 10 cm

Instructions:

With larger hook and White, ch 34.

Row 1: Work 1 sc in 2nd ch from hook, work 1 sc in every ch across = 33 dc; turn.
Row 2: Ch 1, 1 sc in back loop of each sc across = 33 dc; turn.
Row 3: Work as for Row 2.
Row 4: Change to Beige and work as for Row 2.
Row 5: Work as for Row 2.
Row 6: Change to White and work as for Row 2.
Rows 7 – 9: Work as for Row 2.
Row 10: Change to Beige and work as for Row 2.
Row 11: Work as for Row 2.
Row 12: Change to White and work as for Row 2.
Rows 13 – 15: Work as for Row 2.
Row 16: Change to Beige and Work as for Row 2.
Row 17: Work as for Row 2.
Row 18: Change to White and work as for Row 2.
Rows 19 – 21: Work as for Row 2.
Row 22: Change to Beige and work as for Row 2.
Row 23: Work as for Row 2.
Row 24: Change to White and work as for Row 2.
Rows 25 – 27: Work as for Row 2.
Row 28: Change to Beige and Work as for Row 2.
Row 29: Work as for Row 2.

Row 30: Change to White and work as for Row 2.
Rows 31 – 33: Work as for Row 2.
Row 34: Change to Beige and work as for Row 2.
Row 35: Work as for Row 2.
Row 36: Change to White and work as for Row 2.
Rows 37 – 38: Work as for Row 2.

EDGING:

Rnd 1: Change to smaller hook and White. Attach yarn with 1 sl st in corner, work 3 sc in corner st, 1 sc in each st, 3 sc in corner st.
2nd side: Work 1 sc in each row (make sure the edge doesn't ruffle or pucker) and 3 sc in corner st.
3rd side: Work 1 sc in each ch (= foundation chain), 3 sc in corner st.
4th side: Work 1 sc in each row and end with 1 sl st into 1st sc.
Rnd 2: Work 1 sl st in each sc around, ending 1 sc before last corner. Make a hanging loop in the last corner: Ch 10, skip corner (= 3 sc) and skip next sc; attach loop into next sl st with 1 sl st. Cut yarn and fasten off.

FINISHING: Weave in all ends neatly on WS and gently steam press potholder.

Make another potholder the same way.

Blue for Pleasure

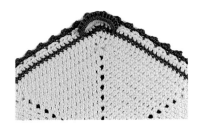

Flower Potholder

MEASUREMENTS:	Approx. 8³/₄ x 8³/₄ in / 22 x 22 cm
MATERIALS:	CYCA #1, Garnstudio Muskat (100% cotton; 109 yd/100 m / 50 g) / Gray-blue 36, 50 g / Off-white 08, 100 g
CROCHET HOOK:	U.S. size D-3 / 3.25 mm
GAUGE:	23 dc in pattern = 4 in / 10 cm

Instructions:

FLOWER:

With Blue, ch 5 and join into a ring with 1 sl st into 1ˢᵗ ch.

Rnd 1: Ch 6 (= 1 dc + 3 ch), *1 dc around ring, ch 3*; rep from * to * 5 times total and end with 1 sl st into 3ʳᵈ ch.

Row 2: (1ˢᵗ petal) 1 sl st around ch loop, 4 sc around ch loop; turn.

Row 3: Ch 1, 1 sc in sc 3 times, 2 sc in same sc; turn.

Row 4: Ch 1, 1 sc in sc 4 times, 2 sc in same sc; turn.

Row 5: Ch 1, 1 sc in sc 5 times, 2 sc in same sc; turn.

Row 6: Ch 1, 1 sc in sc 6 times, 2 sc in same sc; turn.

Row 7: Ch 1, 1 sc in sc 7 times, 2 sc in same sc; turn.

Row 8: Ch 1, 1 sc in sc 9 times; turn.

Row 9: Work as for Row 8.

Row 10: Ch 1, skip 1 sc, 1 sc in sc 8 times; turn.

Row 11: Ch 1, skip 1 sc, 1 sc in sc 7 times; turn.

Row 12: Ch 1, skip 1 sc, 1 sc in sc 6 times; turn.

Row 13: Ch 1, skip 1 sc, 1 sc in sc 5 times; turn.

Row 14: Ch 1, skip 1 sc, 1 sc in sc 4 times; turn.

Row 15: Ch 1, skip 1 sc, 1 sc in sc 3 times; turn.

Row 16: Ch 1, skip 1 sc, 1 sc in sc 2 times; turn.

Cut yarn = 1 petal.

Start a new petal in the next chain loop; repeat **Rows 2 – 16**. Make a petal in each chain loop = 6 petals total.

EDGING AROUND THE FLOWER:

Rnd 1: Change to White. *1 sl st at base of a petal; work 1 sc in each row around the entire petal. Jump directly to the next petal*; rep from * to * until you've crocheted around all the petals. Cut yarn. Weave in all ends and set piece aside.

BACKGROUND:

With White, ch 8 and join into a ring with 1 sl st into 1ˢᵗ ch.

Rnd 1: Ch 5 (= 1 dc + 2 ch), *3 dc around ring, ch 2*; rep from * to * 5 times and end with 2 dc around ring, 1 sl st into 3ʳᵈ ch.

Rnd 2: 1 sl st around ch loop, ch 5 (= 1 dc + 2 ch), 1 dc around ch loop, *1 dc into dc 3 times, (1 dc, ch 2, 1 dc) around ch loop*; rep from * to * around and end with 1 dc in dc 3 times, 1 sl st into 3ʳᵈ ch.

Rnd 3: 1 sl st around ch loop, ch 5 (= 1 dc + 2 ch), 1 dc around ch loop, *1 dc into dc 5 times, (1 dc, ch 2, 1 dc) around ch loop*; rep from * to * around and end with 1 dc in dc 5 times, 1 sl st into 3ʳᵈ ch.

Rnd 4: 1 sl st around ch loop, ch 5 (= 1 dc + 2 ch), 1 dc around ch loop, *1 dc into dc 7 times, (1 dc, ch 2, 1 dc) around ch loop*; rep from * to * around and end with 1 dc in dc 7 times, 1 sl st into 3ʳᵈ ch.

Rnd 5: 1 sl st around ch loop, ch 5 (= 1 dc + 2 ch), 1 dc around ch loop, *1 dc into dc 9 times, (1 dc, ch 2, 1 dc) around ch loop*; rep from * to * around and end with 1 dc in dc 9 times, 1 sl st into 3ʳᵈ ch.

Rnd 6: 1 sl st around ch loop, ch 5 (= 1 dc + 2 ch), 1 dc around ch loop, *1 dc into dc 11 times, (1 dc, ch 2, 1 dc) around ch loop*; rep from * to * around and end with 1 dc in dc 11 times, 1 sl st into 3ʳᵈ ch.

Rnd 7: 1 sl st around ch loop, ch 5 (= 1 dc + 2 ch), 1 dc around ch loop, *1 dc into dc 13 times, (1 dc, ch 2, 1 dc) around ch loop*; rep from * to * around and end with 1 dc in dc 13 times, 1 sl st into 3ʳᵈ ch.

Rnd 8: 1 sl st around ch loop, ch 5 (= 1 dc + 2 ch), 1 dc around ch loop, *1 dc into dc 15 times, (1 dc, ch 2, 1 dc) around ch loop*; rep from * to * around and end with 1 dc in dc 15 times, 1 sl st into 3ʳᵈ ch.

Rnd 9: Join the flower to the background on this round: 1 sl st around ch loop, ch 4 (= 1 dc + 1 ch), 1 sl st into top of a petal, ch 1, 1 dc around ch loop, *1 dc into dc 17 times, (1 dc, ch 1, 1 sl st) in top of next petal, ch 1, 1 dc*; rep from * to * around and end with 1 dc in dc 17 times, 1 sl st into 3ʳᵈ ch.

Rnd 10: 1 sl st around ch loop, 1 sl st into sl st, ch 3, 2 dc into

same sl st, *1 dc into dc 19 times, skip 1 ch, 3 dc into sl st, skip 1 ch*; rep from * to * around and end with skip 1 ch, 3 dc in sl st, skip 1 ch, 1 dc into dc 19 times, 1 sl st into 3rd ch.

Rnd 11: 1 sl st into ch, *3 sc in next dc, 1 sc in dc 21 times*; rep from * to * around and end with 1 sl st into 1st sc. Change to Blue, bringing Blue yarn through sl st.

Rnd 12: *3 sc in next sc, 1 sc in sc 23 times*; rep from * to * around and end with 1 sl st into 1st sc. Change to White, bringing new yarn through sl st.

Rnd 13: 1 sl st into next sc, ch 2, 1 hdc in same sc as sl sl, *1 hdc in sc 25 times, 2 hdc in next sc*; rep from * to * around and end with 1 hdc in sc 25 times. 1 sl st in 2nd ch. Change to Blue, bringing Blue through sl st.

Rnd 14: Ch 1, *1 sc in hdc, ch 3, 1 sc in 1st ch (= picot), skip 2 hdc*; rep from * to * around and end with 1 sl st in ch. Cut yarn.

HANGING LOOP:
Crochet loop to back side of background. With Blue, attach yarn with sl st around 4th sc before a corner. Ch 12 and attach loop with 1 sl st to 4th sc past corner; turn and work 14 sc around ch loop; end with 1 sl st into sl st.

FINISHING: Weave in all ends neatly on WS and gently steam press potholder.

Make another potholder the same way.

Spiral Potholder

MEASUREMENTS:	Approx. 8 in / 20 cm diameter
MATERIALS:	CYCA #1, Garnstudio Muskat (100% cotton; 109 yd/100 m / 50 g) / Gray-blue 36, 50 g / Off-white 08, 50 g
CROCHET HOOK:	U.S. size D-3 / 3.25 mm
GAUGE:	9 rounds in sc = 4 in / 10 cm in diameter

Instructions:

With White, ch 7 and join into a ring with 1 sl st into 1st ch.

The potholder is worked in a continual spiral with no ending st on the round. Always carry both colors and catch the unused yarn with the working yarn on every stitch. For more on how to catch yarn not in use and how to change colors, see page 109.

Rnd 1: Ch 1, *2 sc with White, 2 sc with Blue around ring*; rep from * to * 4 times; 1 sc in next sc. Begin next rnd. On this and all following rnds, shift by 1 sc to produce the spiral pattern. *At the same time*, there are 8 sts increased per round.

Rnd 2: *With White, 1 sc in sc, 2 sc in next sc; change to Blue, 1 sc in sc, 2 sc in next sc*; rep from * to * 4 times, 1 sc into next sc.

Rnd 3: *With White, 1 sc in sc 2 times, 2 sc in next sc; change to Blue, 1 sc in sc 2 times, 2 sc in next sc*; rep from * to * 4 times, 1 sc into next sc.

Rnd 4: *With White, 1 sc in sc 3 times, 2 sc in next sc; change to Blue, 1 sc in sc 3 times, 2 sc in next sc*; rep from * to * 4 times, 1 sc into next sc.

Rnd 5: *With White, 1 sc in sc 4 times, 2 sc in next sc; change to Blue, 1 sc in sc 4 times, 2 sc in next sc*; rep from * to * 4 times, 1 sc into next sc.

Rnds 6 – 16: Work as for Rnd 5 with 1 sc more between each increase = 8 increases per round.

Rnd 17: *With White, 1 sc in sc 16 times, 2 sc in next sc; change to Blue, 1 sc in sc 16 times, 2 sc in next sc*; rep from * to * 4 times, 1 sc into next sc.

Rnd 18: Work entire round with Blue, with 1 sc in each sc around.

Rnd 19: Work entire round with White, with 1 sc in each sc around. Cut yarn.

EDGING:

With Blue, *2 sc in the same sc, ch 3, 1 sc into 1st ch (= 1 picot), skip 2 sc*; rep from * to * around.

HANGING LOOP:

Continue with Blue to make the hanging loop: ch 14, join with 1 sl st into 1st sc; turn and work 16 sc around ch loop; end with 1 sl st into nearest sc.

FINISHING:

Weave in all ends neatly on WS.

Make another potholder the same way.

Simple Flower Potholder

MEASUREMENTS:	Approx. 8 3/4 x 8 3/4 in / 22 x 22 cm diameter
MATERIALS:	CYCA #1, Garnstudio Muskat (100% cotton; 109 yd/100 m / 50 g) / Gray-blue 36, 50 g / Off-white 08, 50 g
CROCHET HOOK:	U.S. size D-3 / 3.25 mm
GAUGE:	23 dc = 4 in / 10 cm in diameter

Instructions:

Circle in the Center:

With White, ch 7 and join into a ring with 1 sl st into 1st ch.

Rnd 1: Ch 3 (= 1 dc), work 16 dc around ring and end with 1 sl st to 3rd ch.

Rnd 2: Ch 7 (= 1 dc + 4 ch), *skip 1 dc, 1 dc into dc, ch 4*; rep from * to * around and end with ch 4.

Rnd 3: Ch 1, *5 sc around ch loop, 1 sc into dc*; rep from * to * around and end with 1 sl st into ch.

Rnd 4: Ch 11 (= 1 dc + 8 ch), *skip 5 sc, 1 dc in sc, ch 8*; rep from * to * around and end with ch 10, 1 sl st into 3rd ch.

Rnd 5: Ch 1, *(1 sc, 2 hdc, 5 dc, 2 hdc, 1 sc) into ch loop, skip 1 dc*; rep from * to * around and end with 1 sl st into ch. Cut yarn and weave in yarn tail on WS. Set piece aside.

BACKGROUND:

With White, ch 7 and join into a ring with 1 sl st into 1st ch.

Rnd 1: Ch 1, work 12 sc around ring and end with 1 st st to ch.

Rnd 2: Ch 3 (= 1 dc), 1 dc into same sc, *2 dc in dc*; rep from * to * around and end with 1 sl st into 3rd ch = 24 dc.

Rnd 3: Ch 3 (= 1 dc), 1 dc in same st, *1 dc into dc, 2 dc into next dc*; rep from * to * around and end with 1 sl st into 3rd ch = 36 dc.

Rnd 4: Ch 3 (= 1 dc), 1 dc in same st, *1 dc into each of next 2 dc, 2 dc into next dc*; rep from * to * around and end with 1 sl st into 3rd ch = 48 dc.

Rnd 5: Ch 3 (= 1 dc), 1 dc in same st, *1 dc into each of next 3 dc, 2 dc into next dc*; rep from * to * around and end with 1 sl st into 3rd ch = 60 dc.

Rnd 6: Ch 3 (= 1 dc), 1 dc in same st, *1 dc into each of next 4 dc, 2 dc into next dc*; rep from * to * around and end with 1 sl st into 3rd ch = 72 dc.

Rnd 7: Ch 3 (= 1 dc), 1 dc in same st, *1 dc into each of next 5 dc, 2 dc into next dc*; rep from * to * around and end with 1 sl st into 3rd ch = 84 dc.

Rnd 8: Change to Blue by bringing yarn through the last step of the sl st on the previous rnd. Ch 3 (= 1 dc), 1 dc in same st, *1 dc into each of next 6 dc, 2 dc into next dc*; rep from * to * around and end with 1 sl st into 3rd ch = 96 dc.

Rnd 9: Change to White. Ch 3 (= 1 dc), 1 dc in same st, *1 dc into each of next 7 dc, 2 dc into next dc*; rep from * to * around and end with 1 sl st into 3rd ch = 108 dc. Cut yarn.

EDGING:

Change to Blue. Ch 1, *1 sc in dc, ch 3, 1 sc into 1st ch (= picot), skip 1 dc*; rep from * to * around and end with 1 sl st into ch. Do not cut yarn; continue with hanging loop.

HANGING LOOP:

Ch 15 and secure with 1 sl st to sl st on edge, work 20 sc around loop and end with 1 sl st. Cut yarn.

FINISHING:

Weave in all ends neatly on WS. Center the circle on the background and sew it securely to the background at the tip of each "petal." Gently steam press potholder.

Make another potholder the same way.

Dress Potholder, Large

MEASUREMENTS: Length, Approx. 7 in / 18 cm; width of skirt, approx. 8 in / 20 cm

MATERIALS: CYCA #1, PT Petunia (100% cotton; 120 yd/110 m / 50 g) / Blue 275, 50 g / White 221, 100 g

CROCHET HOOK: U.S. size C-2 or D-3 / 3 mm

GAUGE: 20 dc = 4 in / 10 cm

Instructions:

YOKE:
With Blue, ch 22.

Row 1: Beg in the 2nd ch from hook, work 1 sc in each ch (= 21 sc); turn.

Row 2: Ch 1, 1 sc in each sc across (= 21 sc); turn.

Rows 3 – 26: Work as for Row 2. Cut yarn.

SKIRT:
Rnd 1: With White, attach yarn to 1st sc of row, ch 5 (= 1 dc + 2 ch), *skip 1 sc, 1 dc in next sc, ch 2*; rep from * to * across and end with 1 dc (fold the yoke in half and) continue around the foundation chain as follows: 1 dc, rep from * to * along foundation chain and end with 1 dc and then 1 sl st into 3rd ch.

Rnd 2: 1 sl st around ch loop, ch 3 (= 1 dc), 1 dc around loop, ch 2, 2 dc around same loop, *(2 dc, ch 2, 2 dc) around next ch loop*; rep from * to * around and end with 1 sl st into 3rd ch.

Rnd 3: 1 sl st into dc, 1 sl st around ch loop, ch 3, 1 dc around loop, ch 2, 2 dc in same loop, *(2 dc, ch 2, 2 dc) around next ch loop*; rep from * to * and end with 1 sl st into 3rd ch.

Rnds 4 – 10: Work as for Rnd 3.

Rnd 11: Change to Blue and work as for Rnd 3.

Rnd 12: Change to White and work as for Rnd 3.

Rnd 13: Change to Blue and work as for Rnd 3. Cut yarn.

ARMHOLE EDGING:
With White: Beg at base of armhole, attaching yarn with 1 sl st. Work 1 sc between 2 rows, *ch 3, sl st into 1st ch (= picot), skip 2 rows, 1 sc*; rep from * to * around entire armhole. Work the armhole on the other side the same way.

HANGING LOOP:
With White: Attach yarn with 1 sl st 2 sc from the center of the top of the yoke. Ch 6, skip 4 sc and attach with 1 sl st; turn and work 10 sc around loop, cut yarn and weave in end on WS.

TIE FOR WAIST:
With Blue: Crochet a chain 19³/₄ in / 50 cm long. Thread the cord through the waist = 1st rnd of skirt and tie into a bow (see photo).

FINISHING: Weave in all ends neatly on WS and lightly steam press potholder.

Make another potholder the same way.

Dress Potholder, Small

MEASUREMENTS:	Length, approx. 6 in / 15 cm; width of skirt, approx. 5½ in / 14 cm
MATERIALS:	CYCA #1, PT Petunia (100% cotton; 120 yd/110 m / 50 g) / Blue 275, 50 g / Beige 220, 50 g
CROCHET HOOK:	U.S. size C-2 or D-3 / 3 mm
GAUGE:	20 dc = 4 in / 10 cm

Instructions:

YOKE:

With Beige, ch 17.

Row 1: Beg in the 2nd ch from hook, work 1 sc in each ch (= 16 sc); turn.

Row 2: Ch 1, 1 sc in back loop of each sc across (= 16 sc); turn.

Rows 3 – 24: Work as for Row 2. Do not cut yarn; continue with skirt.

SKIRT:

Rnd 1: Ch 3 (= 1 dc), 1 dc in next st, *ch 2, skip 1 sc, 1 dc in each of next 2 sc,*; rep from * to * across. Fold the yoke in half and continue around the foundation chain: rep from * to * along foundation chain and end with ch 2, and then 1 sl st into 3rd ch.

Rnd 2: 1 sl st in dc 2 times, 1 sl st around ch loop, ch 3 (= 1 dc), 2 dc around ch loop, ch 3, 3 dc around same loop, *skip 2 dc, (3 dc, ch 3, 3 dc) around next ch loop*; rep from * to * around and end with 1 sl st into 3rd ch.

Rnd 3: 1 sl st into dc 2 times, 1 sl st around ch loop, ch 3 (= 1 dc), 2 dc around loop, ch 3, 3 dc around same loop, *(3 dc, ch 3, 3 dc) around next ch loop*; rep from * to * and end with 1 sl st into 3rd ch.

Rnds 4 – 7: Work as for Rnd 3.

Rnd 8: Change to Blue and work as for Rnd 3.

Rnd 9: Change to Beige and work as for Rnd 3.

ARMHOLE EDGING:

With Blue: Beg at base of armhole, attaching yarn with 1 sl st. Work 1 sc between 2 rows, *ch 3, sl st into 1st ch (= picot), skip 2 rows, 1 sc*; rep from * to * around entire armhole. Work the armhole on the other side the same way.

HANGING LOOP:

With Blue: Attach yarn with 1 sl st 2 sc from the center of the top of the yoke. Ch 6, skip 4 sc and attach with 1 sl st; turn and work 10 sc around loop, cut yarn and weave in end on WS.

TIE FOR WAIST:

With Blue: Crochet a chain 17¾ in / 45 cm long. Thread the cord through the waist = 1st rnd of skirt and tie into a bow (see photo).

FINISHING: Weave in all ends neatly on WS and lightly steam press potholder.

Make another potholder the same way.

Color Joy

Rose Potholder

MEASUREMENTS:	Approx. 7³/₄ x 7³/₄ in / 19.5 x 19.5 cm
MATERIALS:	CYCA #1, PT Petunia (100% cotton; 120 yd/110 m / 50 g) / Rose 248, 50 g / Green 215, 50 g / White 221, 100 g
CROCHET HOOK:	U.S. sizes C-2 or D-3 + E-4 / 3 and 3.5 mm (larger size is used for foundation chain on back)
GAUGE:	20 dc with smaller hook = 4 in / 10 cm

Instructions:

CROCHETED ROSE:

With Rose and smaller hook, ch 5 and join into a ring with 1 sl st into 1st ch.

Rnd 1: Ch 6 (= 1 dc + ch 3), (1 dc around ring, ch 3) 7 times and end with 1 sl st into 3rd ch.

Rnd 2: *(1 sc, ch 1, 3 dc, ch 1, 1 sc) around ch-3 loop = 1 petal*; work from * to * 8 times total and end with 1 st st into 1st sc.

Rnd 3: *1 sc on dc from 1st rnd (crochet around the dc behind the petal), ch 4, 1 sc on dc from 1st rnd*; work from * to * 8 times total and end with 1 sl st into 1st sc.

Rnd 4: Ch 1, *(1 sc, ch 2, 5 dc, ch 2, 1 sc) around ch-4 loop*; work from * to * 8 times total and end with 1 st st into 1st sc.

Rnd 5: *1 sc on sc from 3rd rnd (crochet around the sc), ch 5, 1 sc on sc from 3rd rnd*; work from * to * 8 times total and end with 1 sl st into 1st sc.

Rnd 6: Ch 1, *(1 hdc, 2 dc, 3 tr, 2 dc, 1 hdc) around ch-5 loop*; work from * to * 8 times total and end with 1 st st into 1st hdc.

Rnd 7: *1 sc on sc from 5th rnd (crochet around the sc), ch 6, 1 sc on sc from 5th rnd*; work from * to * 8 times total and end with 1 sl st into 1st sc.

Rnd 8: Ch 1, *(1 hdc, 2 dc, 5 tr, 2 dc, 1 hdc) around ch-6 loop*; work from * to * 8 times total and end with 1 st st into 1st hdc. Cut yarn and weave in end on WS.

LEAVES:

With Green, attach yarn with 1 sl st into 1st hdc of a petal. Ch 7, 1 sc in 2nd ch from hook, 1 dc in each of the next 5 ch, end the first leaf with 1 sl st into 1st tr of petal. Ch 9, 1 dc in the 4th ch from hook, 1 dc in each of the next 5 ch and end the second leaf with 1 sl st into the 5th tr of petal. Ch 7, 1 sc in 2nd ch from hook, 1 dc in each of the next 5 ch and end with 3rd leaf with 1 sl st into the last hdc of petal. Cut yarn and weave in end. Crochet 3 leaves on every alternate petal around (see photo).

EDGING AROUND ROSE AND LEAVES:

Rnd 1: With White, attach yarn with 1 sl st into 3rd tr of a petal. Ch 4 (= 1 tr), *ch 5, 1 sc in top of 1st leaf, ch 5, 1 sc in 4th dc of 2nd leaf, ch 4, 1 sc in top of leaf, ch 4, 1 sc in 4th dc of opposite side of leaf, ch 5, 1 sc in top of 3rd leaf, ch 5, 1 tr in 3rd tr of next petal*; work from * to * 4 times total. On the last repeat, omit the last tr and end with 1 st st into 4th ch.

Rnd 2: Ch 4, 1 sc around ch loop, ch 4, *1 sc around next ch loop, ch 4*; rep from * to * around and end by skipping 4 ch and then work 1 sl st into 1st ch.

Rnd 3: 1 sl st into ch loop, ch 3 (= 1 dc), 3 dc around same loop, *ch 1, 4 dc on next ch loop*; rep from * to * around and end with 1 sl st into 3rd ch.

Rnd 4: 1 sl st in each of the next 3 dc, 1 sl st around ch loop, ch 3 (= 1 dc), 1 dc, ch 3, 2 dc around same loop, skip 4 dc, *(2 dc, ch 3, 2 dc) around same loop, skip 4 dc*; rep from * to * once, ch 4 (corner), skip 4 dc; rep from * to * and ch 4 at each corner around. End with 1 sl st into 3rd ch. Cut yarn and weave in end on WS.

Rnd 5: With Rose, attach yarn to a corner ch loop with sl st. Ch 3 (= 1 dc), 8 dc around same corner loop, skip 2 dc, 5 dc around next loop, *skip 4 dc, 5 dc around next loop*; rep from * to * to next corner. Skip 2 dc, 9 dc around corner loop, skip 2 dc; rep from * to * to next corner, work corner, and rep around. End with 1 sl st into 3rd ch. Cut yarn and weave in end on WS.

BACK:

With White and larger hook, ch 42.

Row 1: Change to smaller hook. Beg in 4th ch from hook, work 1 dc in each ch across; turn.

Row 2: Ch 3 (= 1 dc), work 1 dc in each dc across = 39 dc; turn.

Rows 3 – 22: Work as for Row 2. Cut yarn and weave in end on WS.

JOINING:

With White and smaller hook: With WS facing WS, join the back to the front beg at one corner. Attach yarn with sl st through both layers. (Ch 3, 1 sl st into 1st ch (= 1 picot), skip 1 dc on front and back, 1 sl st through both layers) 5 times. Insert hook down through the 1st and 2nd dc on Rnd 4 of the front and skip 1 dc on the back. Work 1 sc through both layers, *ch 3, 1 sl st into 1st ch (= 1 picot), skip 1 dc on front and back, 1 sl st through both layers), rep sts in parentheses 3 times. Insert hook down through the 2nd and 3rd dc on Rnd 4 of the front and skip 1 dc on the back. Work 1 sc through both layers*; rep from * to * down the side. Now repeat the corner as explained above and then rep * to * on the next side, working through the front on every row and skipping a dc on the back as before. Repeat the sequence on the last two sides.

HANGING LOOP:

With White, attach yarn with 1 sl st on the back 3/8 in / 1 cm in from a corner. Ch 6, skip approx. 3/4 in / 2 cm diagonally and attach chain with 1 sl st to back 3/8 in / 1 cm from corner; turn and work 10 sc around loop. Cut yarn and weave in ends neatly on WS.

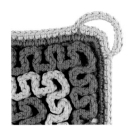

Ruffled Potholder
on Filet Base

MEASUREMENTS:	Approx. 8 x 8 in / 20 x 20 cm
MATERIALS:	Filet base: CYCA #1, PT Pandora (100% cotton; 180 yd/165 m / 50 g) / Pink 251, 50 g
TOP:	CYCA #1, PT Petunia (100% cotton; 120 yd/110 m / 50 g) / Light pink 200, 100 g / Pink 248 100 g
CROCHET HOOK:	U.S size B-1 or C-2 / 2.5 mm for filet base and U.S. D-3 / 3 mm for foundation chain and top "ruffles")
GAUGE:	36 sts with smaller hook = 4 in / 10 cm

Instructions:

FILET BASE:
With larger hook and Pink Pandora yarn, ch 68.

Row 1: Change to smaller hook. Work 1 edc (extended double crochet) in the 8th ch from hook, *ch 2, skip 2 ch, 1 edc*; rep from * to * 20 times (= 21 filet blocks); turn.
Row 2: Ch 5 (= 1 edc + 2 ch), *1 edc in next edc, ch 2*; rep from * to * 20 times, ch 2, 1 edc in last edc.
Rows 3 – 21: Work as for Row 2 (= 21 filet blocks in length); cut yarn and weave in end on WS.

TOP (RUFFLES):
Rnd 1: With larger hook and Pink Petunia yarn, begin at center of the filet base. Attach the yarn with 1 sl st on 1 dc of the block, ch 3 (= 1 dc), work 3 dc around each dc or every ch-2 loop (see drawing and the arrows indicating sequence for crocheting the ruffles). End each ruffle round with 1 st sl into 3rd ch.
Rnd 2: With Light Pink and larger hook, work round as indicated on drawing.
Rnd 3: With Pink and larger hook, work round as indicated on drawing.
Rnd 4: With Light Pink and larger hook, work round as indicated on drawing.
Rnd 5: With Pink and larger hook, work round as indicated on drawing.

EDGING:
Rnd 1: With Pink and smaller hook, work 5 sc in each corner and 1 sc in edc, 2 sc in block along the sides. End rnd with 1 sl st into 1st sc; cut yarn.

Rnd 2: Change to Light Pink. Begin at the center of a long side and work 1 sc in every sc; in each corner work 2 sc in each of the 3 center sc so the corners are rounded.

Note: The hanging loop is also worked on this round as follows: work 2 sc past the last corner, ch 12 and then 1 sl st into the 3rd sc before the corner; work 13 sc around ch loop and then continue with 1 sc in the next sc along the edge; end with 1 sl st into 1st sc.

FINISHING: Weave in all ends neatly on WS and lightly steam press potholder on back only.

Filet Base

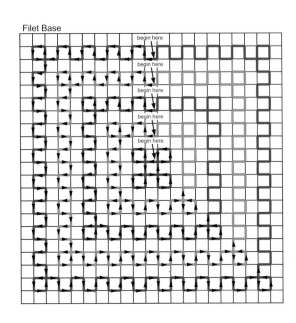

Sometimes you don't have the right size yarn for the potholders but, if you crochet with a thinner yarn and double the strands, you will have many options. If you crochet with a doubled strand of yarn, you can also make "your own colors" by blending two colors as we've done with these potholders.

Round Potholder with Bobbles

MEASUREMENTS:	Approx. 8½ in / 21.5 cm diameter
MATERIALS:	CYCA #2, Garnstudio Safran (100% cotton; 176 yd/161 m / 50 g) / Beige 21, 50 g / Light Pink 16, 50 g / Pink 13, 50 g
CROCHET HOOK:	U.S. size G-6 / 4 mm
GAUGE:	18 dc = 4 in / 10 cm

Instructions:

With 2 strands of Light Pink held together, ch 7 and join into a ring with 1 st st into 1st ch.

Rnd 1: Ch 1, work 12 sc around ring; end with 1 sl st into ch.
Rnd 2: Ch 3 (= 1 dc) and work 1 dc in same sc, *2 dc into next dc*; rep from * to * around and end with 1 sl st into 3rd ch = 24 dc.
Rnd 3: Change to 2 strands of Beige (see how to change colors on page 109). Ch 3 (= 1 dc), 1 dc in same dc, *1 dc in dc, 2 dc in next dc*; rep from * to * around and end with 1 sl st into 3rd ch = 36 dc.
Rnd 4: Ch 3 (= 1 dc), 1 dc in same dc, *1 dc in each of next 2 dc, 2 dc in next dc*; rep from * to * around and end with 1 sl st into 3rd ch = 48 dc.
Rnd 5: Change to 1 strand each Beige and Light Pink. Ch 3 (= 1 dc), 1 dc in same dc, *1 dc in each of next 3 dc, 2 dc in next dc*; rep from * to * around and end with 1 sl st into 3rd ch = 60 dc.
Rnd 6: Change to 2 strands Pink. Ch 3 (= 1 dc), 1 dc in same dc, *1 dc in each of next 4 dc, 2 dc in next dc*; rep from * to * around and end with 1 sl st into 3rd ch = 72 dc.
Rnd 7: Ch 3 (= 1 dc), 1 dc in same dc, *1 dc in each of next 5 dc, 2 dc in next dc*; rep from * to * around and end with 1 sl st into 3rd ch = 84 dc.

Rnd 8: Change to 2 strands Light Pink. Ch 1 (= 1 sc), 1 sc in each dc around and end with 1 sl st into 1 st ch = 84 sc.
Rnd 9: Ch 1 (= 1 sc), *1 sc in next sc, 1 bobble (= 4 dc in the same st and joined on last step—see page 116), 1 sc in next sc*; rep from * to * around and end with 1 sl st into 1st ch = 84 sc.
Rnd 10: Ch 1 (= 1 sc), 1 sc in same sc, *1 sc in each of next 6 sc, 2 sc in next sc*; rep from * to * around and end with 1 sl st into ch = 96 sc.
Rnd 11: Change to 2 strands Pink, ch 3 (= 1 dc), 1 dc in same sc, *1 dc in each of next 7 sc, 2 dc in next sc*; rep from * to * around and end with 1 sl st into 3rd ch = 108 dc.
Rnd 12: Change to 2 strands Beige. Ch 2 (= 1 hdc), 1 hdc in same dc, *1 hdc in each of next 8 dc, 2 hdc in next dc*; rep from * to * around and end with 1 sl st into 3rd ch = 120 hdc.
Rnd 13: 1 sl st into each hdc around and end with 1 sl st into sl st. Continue directly to hanging loop with ch 10, skip 6 sl sts, work 1 sl st into next sl st; turn and work 1 sl st into each ch. End with 1 sl st into 1st sl st. Cut yarn.

FINISHING: Weave in all ends neatly on WS and lightly steam press potholder on back only.

Make another potholder the same way.

Hexagonal Potholder in Multi-colored Pastels

MEASUREMENTS:	Approx. 8¼ x 8¼ in / 21 x 21 cm
MATERIALS:	CYCA #2, Garnstudio Safran (100% cotton; 176 yd/161 m / 50 g) / Natural White 18, 50 g / Light Pink 16, 50 g / Pink 13, 50 g
CROCHET HOOK:	U.S. size G-6 / 4 mm
GAUGE:	18 dc = 4 in / 10 cm

Instructions:

With 1 strand each White and Light Pink, ch 8 and join into a ring with 1 sl st into 1st ch.

Rnd 1: Ch 5 (= 1 dc + ch 2), *2 dc around ring, ch 2*; rep from * to * 5 times and end with 1 dc around ring, 1 sl st into 3rd ch.

Rnd 2: 1 sl st around ch loop, ch 5 (= 1 dc + ch 2), 1 dc around ch loop, *1 dc into each of next 2 dc, (1 dc, ch 2, 1 dc) around next ch loop*; rep from * to * around and end with 1 dc in each of next 2 dc, 1 sl st into 3rd ch.

Rnd 3: Change to 2 strands Light Pink. 1 sl st around ch loop, ch 5 (= 1 dc + ch 2), 1 dc around ch loop, *1 dc into each of next 4 dc, (1 dc, ch 2, 1 dc) around next ch loop*; rep from * to * around and end with 1 dc in each of next 4 dc, 1 sl st into 3rd ch.

Rnd 4: 1 sl st around ch loop, ch 5 (= 1 dc + ch 2), 1 dc around ch loop, *1 dc into each of next 6 dc, (1 dc, ch 2, 1 dc) around next ch loop*; rep from * to * around and end with 1 dc in each of next 6 dc, 1 sl st into 3rd ch.

Rnd 5: Change to 1 strand each White and Light Pink. 1 sl st around ch loop, ch 5 (= 1 dc + ch 2), 1 dc around ch loop, *1 dc into each of next 8 dc, (1 dc, ch 2, 1 dc) around next ch loop*; rep from * to * around and end with 1 dc in each of next 8 dc, 1 sl st into 3rd ch.

Rnd 6: Change to 1 strand each Light Pink and Pink. 1 sl st around ch loop, ch 5 (= 1 dc + ch 2), 1 dc around ch loop, *1 dc into each of next 10 dc, (1 dc, ch 2, 1 dc) around next ch loop*; rep from * to * around and end with 1 dc in each of next 10 dc, 1 sl st into 3rd ch.

Rnd 7: Change to 2 strands Pink. 1 sl st around ch loop, ch 5 (= 1 dc + ch 2), 1 dc around ch loop, *1 dc into each of next 12 dc, (1 dc, ch 2, 1 dc) around next ch loop*; rep from * to * around and end with 1 dc in each of next 12 dc, 1 sl st into 3rd ch.

Rnd 8: Change to 1 strand each Light Pink and Pink. 1 sl st around ch loop, ch 5 (= 1 dc + ch 2), 1 dc around ch loop, *1 dc into each of next 14 dc, (1 dc, ch 2, 1 dc) around next ch loop*; rep from * to * around and end with 1 dc in each of next 14 dc, 1 sl st into 3rd ch.

Rnd 9: Change to 1 strand each White and Pink. 1 sl st around ch loop, ch 5 (= 1 dc + ch 2), 1 dc around ch loop, *1 dc into each of next 16 dc, (1 dc, ch 2, 1 dc) around next ch loop*; rep from * to * around and end with 1 dc in each of next 16 dc, 1 sl st into 3rd ch.

Rnd 10: Change to 2 strands White. 1 sl st around ch loop, ch 4 (= 1 hdc + ch 2), 1 hdc around ch loop, *1 hdc in each of next 18 dc, (1 hdc, ch 1, 1 hdc) around next ch loop*; rep from * to * around and end with 1 hdc in each of next 18 dc, 1 sl st into 3rd ch.

EDGING:

Rnd 1: Change to 2 strands Light Pink. Begin at a corner with a ch-2 loop, work 1 crab st over each hdc and ch-2 loop around. The round is worked from left to right. End rnd with 1 sl st into ch-2 loop and continue with the hanging loop.

HANGING LOOP:

Ch 14, 1 sl st around ch-2 loop, work 16 sc around loop and end with 1 sl st into the last crab st. cut yarn and fasten off.

FINISHING: Weave in all ends neatly on WS and lightly steam press potholder.

Make another potholder the same way.

Potholder with Ruffled Edging

MEASUREMENTS:	Approx. 7½ in / 19 cm diameter
MATERIALS:	CYCA #2, Garnstudio Safran (100% cotton; 176 yd/161 m / 50 g) / Beige 21, 50 g / Pink 13, 50 g
CROCHET HOOK:	U.S. size D-3 / 3.25 mm
GAUGE:	26 dc = 4 in / 10 cm

Instructions:

With Beige, ch 8 and join into a ring with 1 sl st into 1st ch.

Rnd 1: Ch 3 (= 1 dc), work 23 dc around ring and end with 1 sl st into 3rd ch = 24 dc.

Rnd 2: Ch 3 (= 1 dc), *ch 1, 1 dc in next dc*; rep from * to * around and end with 1 sl st into 3rd ch = 24 dc.

Rnd 3: 1 sl st around ch loop, ch 3 (= 1 dc), *ch 1, 1 dc around ch loop*; rep from * to * around and end with 1 sl st into 3rd ch = 24 dc.

Rnd 4: 1 sl st into dc, 1 sl st around ch loop, ch 3 (= 1 dc), 1 dc around same loop, *ch 1, skip 1 dc, 2 dc around loop*; rep from * to * around and end with ch 1, skip 1 dc, 1 sl st into 3rd ch.

Rnd 5: Work as for Rnd 4.

Rnd 6: 1 sl st into dc, 1 sl st around ch loop, ch 3 (= 1 dc), 1 dc around same loop, *ch 1, skip 2 dc, 3 dc around loop*; rep from * to * around and end with ch 1, skip 2 dc, 1 sl st into 3rd ch. Cut yarn.

Rnd 7: Change to Pink. 1 sl st around ch loop, ch 3 (= 1 dc), 2 dc around loop, ch 2, 3 dc around same loop, *skip 3 dc, ch 1, (3 dc, ch 2, 3 dc) around next loop*; rep from * to * around and end with 1 sl st into 3rd ch.

Rnd 8: Ch 3 (= 1 dc), 1 dc in each of next 2 dc, (3 dc, ch 2, 3 dc) around next ch loop, 1 dc in each of next 3 dc, ch 1, *1 dc in each of next 3 dc, (3 dc, ch 2, 3 dc) around next ch loop, 1 dc in each of next 3 dc, ch 1*; rep from * to * around and end with 1 sl st into 3rd ch.

Rnd 9: Ch 3 (= 1 dc), 1 dc in each of next 5 dc, (3 dc, ch 2, 3 dc) around next ch loop, 1 dc in each of next 6 dc, ch 1, *1 dc in each of next 6 dc, (3 dc, ch 2, 3 dc) around next ch loop, 1 dc in each of next 5 dc, ch 1*; rep from * to * around and end with 1 sl st into 3rd ch.

Rnd 10: Ch 3 (= 1 dc), 1 dc in each of next 8 dc, (3 dc, ch 1, 3 dc) around next ch loop, 1 dc in each of next 9 dc, ch 1, *1 dc in each of next 6 dc, (3 dc, ch 1, 3 dc) around next ch loop, 1 dc in each of next 8 dc, ch 1*; rep from * to * around and end with 1 sl st into 3rd ch.

Rnd 11: Change to Beige. Ch 1, work 1 sc in each dc and ch loop around; end with 1 sl st into 1st ch.

Rnd 12: Ch 1, work 1 sc in each sc around, while, *at the same time*, making the ruffled edge as follows: Work in sc until 10 sc past the center of the second chevron and skip back to the first chevron and 10 sc past the center of the chevron; *remove hook from st, insert the hook through the st of the previous chevron and catch the yarn; pull through both sts. Continue to sc on the next chevron to the ch loop of the 10th rnd. Count back 5 sc past the first join of chevrons; crochet the chevron together with 1 sl st. Continue further on the chevron until you come to the next ch loop on the 10th rnd and remove the hook. Count back 5 sc past the last join, insert hook through the st, yarn around hook and work 1 sl st*; rep from * to * around, ending by skipping back on the last chevron as before. *At the same time* attach to the previous chevron with 1 sl st or sew to the last chevron when the yarn is fastened off.

HANGING LOOP:
With Beige, attach yarn with 1 sl st into the join of one of the fan, ch 12, skip to the right and attach the loop with 1 sl st in the next join. Work 15 sc around the loop and end with 1 sl st into sl st.

FINISHING: Weave in all ends neatly on WS and lightly steam press potholder on back only.

Make another potholder the same way.

Purple Flower

MEASUREMENTS:	Approx. 8¼ in / 21 cm diameter
MATERIALS:	CYCA #1, PT Petunia (100% cotton; 120 yd/110 m / 50 g) / Purple 260, 100 g / Beige 220, 50 g
CROCHET HOOK:	U.S. sizes E-4 / 3.5 mm for potholder and C-2 or D-3 / 3 mm for the edging
GAUGE:	22 dc with larger hook = 4 in / 10 cm

Instructions:

With larger hook and Purple, ch 4 and join into a ring with 1 sl st into 1st ch.

Rnd 1: Ch 3 (= 1 dc), work 15 dc around ring and end with 1 sl st into 3rd ch = 16 dc.

Rnd 2: Ch 3 (= 1 dc), 1 dc in the same st as the last sl st, *1 dc in next dc, 2 dc in next dc*; rep from * to * around and end with 1 sl st into 3rd ch = 24 dc.

Row 3: Begin a petal. Ch 11, and, beg in the 2nd ch from the hook, work 1 sc in each ch across, 1 sl st into same sl st as in ring (2nd rnd), ch 1; turn.

Row 4: Along the 10 sc, work 2 sc, 5 dc, 2 tr, work 8 tr in the same sc at the top, continue along the foundation ch of 10 ch and work 2 tr, 5 dc, 2 sc, 1 sl st into sl st, ch 1; turn.

Row 5: Work all around the petal, 4 sc, 5 dc, 2 tr, 3 tr into each of the next 5 tr, 2 tr, 5 dc, 4 sc, 1 sl st in the back loop of the next 2 dc in the ring (2nd rnd) = a completed petal.

Rep Rows 3 – 5: Work each petal separately, making a total of 11 petals.

EDGING:

Change to smaller hook and Beige. Work 1 crab st in each st around each petal, joining from petal to petal. Cut yarn and fasten off.

FINISHING:

Overlap the petals so that they form an even circle and sew together on the back of the potholder (see photo).

HANGING LOOP:

Attach yarn with 1 sl st at the top of a petal, ch 12, skip to top of the next petal and attach with 1 sl st; turn and work 15 sc around loop. End with 1 sl st; cut yarn and fasten off. Weave in all ends neatly on WS.

Make another potholder the same way.

Square Potholder
with Bobbles

MEASUREMENTS:	Approx. 7¼ x 7¼ in / 18.5 x 18.5 cm
MATERIALS:	CYCA #2, Garnstudio Paris (100% cotton; 82 yd/75 m / 50 g) / Natural White 17, 50 g / Pink 59, 50 g/ Dark Pink 60, 100 g
CROCHET HOOK:	U. S. size 7 / 4.5 mm for potholder and U.S. G-6 / 4 mm for edging (last 2 rnds)
GAUGE:	18 sc with larger hook = 4 in / 10 cm

Instructions:

With larger hook and Pink, ch 4 and join into a ring with 1 sl st in 1st ch.

Rnd 1: Ch 1, work 12 sc around ring and end with 1 sl st into ch.

Rnd 2: Ch 1, 1 sc in sc, *3 sc in next sc (= corner), 1 sc into each of next 2 sc*; rep from * to * around and end with 1 sc, 1 sl st into 1st sc.

Rnd 3: Ch 1, 1 sc in each of next 2 sc, *3 sc in next sc (= corner), 1 sc in each of next 4 sc*; rep from * to * around and end with 1 sc in each of next 2 sc, 1 sl st into 1st sc.

Rnd 4: Ch 1, 1 sc in each of next 3 sc, *3 sc in next sc (= corner), 1 sc in each of next 6 sc*; rep from * to * around and end with 1 sc in each of next 3 sc, 1 sl st into 1st sc.

Rnd 5: Ch 1, 1 sc in each of next 4 sc, *3 sc in next sc (= corner), 1 sc in each of next 8 sc*; rep from * to * around and end with 1 sc in each of next 4 sc, 1 sl st into 1st sc.

Rnd 6: Ch 1, 1 sc in each of next 5 sc, *3 sc in next sc (= corner), 1 sc in each of next 10 sc*; rep from * to * around and end with 1 sc in each of next 5 sc, 1 sl st into 1st sc.

Rnd 7: Ch 1, 1 sc in each of next 6 sc, *3 sc in next sc (= corner), 1 sc in each of next 12 sc*; rep from * to * around and end with 1 sc in each of next 6 sc, 1 sl st into 1st sc.

Rnd 8: Change to Natural White. Ch 1 (= 1 sc), 1 sc in each of next 7 sc, *3 sc in next sc (= corner), 1 sc in each of next 14 sc*; rep from * to * around and end with 1 sc in each of next 7 sc, 1 sl st into 1st sc.

Rnd 9: Ch 1, 1 sc in each of next 8 sc, *3 sc in next sc (= corner), 1 sc in each of next 16 sc*; rep from * to * around and end with 1 sc in each of next 8 sc, 1 sl st into 1st sc.

Rnd 10: Change to Pink. Ch 1, 1 sc in each of next 9 sc, *3 sc in next sc (= corner), 1 sc in each of next 18 sc*; rep from * to * around and end with 1 sc in each of next 9 sc, 1 sl st into 1st sc.

Rnd 11: Change to Natural White. Ch 1, 1 sc in each of next 10 sc, *3 sc in next sc (= corner), 1 sc in each of next 20 sc*; rep from * to * around and end with 1 sc in each of next 10 sc, 1 sl st into 1st sc.

Rnd 12: Ch 1, 1 sc in each of next 11 sc, *3 sc in next sc (= corner), 1 sc in each of next 22 sc*; rep from * to * around and end with 1 sc in each of next 11 sc, 1 sl st into 1st sc.

Rnd 13: Change to Dark Pink. Ch 1, 1 sc in each of next 12 sc, *3 sc in next sc (= corner), 1 sc in each of next 24 sc*; rep from * to * around and end with 1 sc in each of next 12 sc, 1 sl st into 1st sc.

Rnd 14: Ch 1, 1 sc in each of next 13 sc, *3 sc in next sc (= corner), 1 sc in each of next 26 sc*; rep from * to * around and end with 1 sc in each of next 13 sc, 1 sl st into 1st sc.

Rnd 15: 1st side: 1 sc, (1 bobble, 1 sc in each of next 2 sc) 4 times, (bobble = 4 dc in the same st, all joined on last step of st – see how to crochet bobbles on page 116), 1 bobble, 3 sc in corner. 2nd side: *(1 bobble, 1 sc in each of next 2 sc) 9 times, 1 bobble, 3 sc in corner*; rep from * to * on 3rd and 4th sides. Last half of 1st side: (1 bobble, 2 sc in each of next 2 sc) 4 times. End with 1 bobble, 1 sc, 1 sl st into ch.

Rnd 16: Change to smaller hook and work 1 sc in each sc and bobble around, with 3 sc in each corner. End with 1 sl st into 1st sc.

Rnd 17: Work 1 sl st into each sc around and end with 1 sl st into 1st sl st.

HANGING LOOP:

Attach Dark Pink with 1 st sl into sl st edge above the 6th bobble on one of the sides. Ch 8, skip backwards to the right above the 5th bobble on the side; remove hook from st and insert it through the sl st and catch the stitch from the chain row; pull st through. Secure to ch row with 1 sl st, work 10 sc around ch loop and end with 1 sl st into sl st.

FINISHING: Weave in all ends neatly on WS and lightly steam press potholder on back only.

Make another potholder the same way.

Jacket Potholder, Small

MEASUREMENTS:	Approx. 7 x 6¼ in / 18 x 16 cm diameter
MATERIALS:	CYCA #1, PT Petunia (100% cotton; 120 yd/110 m / 50 g) / Light Pink 200, 100 g / Purple 260, 50 g
CROCHET HOOK:	U.S. size E-4 / 3.5 mm
GAUGE:	28 sts in pattern = 4 in / 10 cm

Instructions:

BACK:

With Light Pink, ch 31.

Row 1: Beg in the 4th ch from the hook, work 2 dc in next ch, ch 1, skip 1 ch, *1 dc in ch, 2 dc in next ch, ch 1, skip 1 ch*; rep from * to * across and end with 3 dc, ch 1; turn.

Row 2: Ch 3, skip 3 dc, 1 sc in ch, *ch 2, skip 3 dc, 1 sc in ch*; rep from * to * and end with ch 2, skip 3 dc, 1 sc in 3rd ch from previous row; turn.

Row 3: Ch 3 (= 1 dc), 2 dc around ch-2 loop, ch 1, skip 1 ch, *3 dc around ch-2 loop, ch 1, skip 1 ch*; rep from * to * across, ending with 3 dc around ch-3 loop; turn.

Rows 4, 6, 8, 10, 12, 14, 16, 18, 20: Work as for Row 2.

Rows 5, 7, 9, 11, 13, 15, 17, 19: Work as for Row 3.

RIGHT FRONT:

Row 21: Work as for Row 2, but crochet only over 4 dc groups; turn.

Row 22: Work as for Row 3, but crochet only over 4 dc groups; turn.

Rows 23, 25, 27, 29, 31, 33, 35, 37, 39: Work as for Row 21.

Rows 24, 26, 28, 30, 32, 34, 36, 38, 40: Work as for Row 22.

Cut yarn.

LEFT FRONT:

Beg on Row 21, skipping over 2 dc groups (= neck); attach yarn with 1 sl st into ch.

Row 22: Work as for Row 3, but crochet only over 4 dc groups; turn.

Rows 23, 25, 27, 29, 31, 33, 35, 37, 39: Work as for Row 21.

Rows 24, 26, 28, 30, 32, 34, 36, 38, 40: Work as for Row 22.

Cut yarn.

EDGING WORKED IN THE ROUND:

With Purple, attach yarn at lower edge of back in the 1st ch of foundation chain.

Rnd 1: *Ch 2, skip 3 dc, 1 sc in ch*; rep from * to * to the corner; long side: *ch 2, skip 1 dc row, 1 sc around sc*; rep from * to * to next corner, 1 sc in 3rd ch*; continue along lower edge of front as for back to the next corner and end side with 1 sc in the 3rd dc. Next side: work as for long side and neck, 1 sc in ch, ch 2, skip 3 dc, 1 sc in ch; continue on next side as for previous side to the next corner. Crochet lower edge of front as for other front and then continue on next long side. End with 1 sl st into ch.

COLLAR:

Row 1: Count four 3-dc groups down from the shoulder and attach Purple with 1 sl st into 1 ch, 1 sc in ch, 2 hdc in dc, 1 dc in ch, 3 dc in dc. Continue up to and including 3 dc groups past the next shoulder and end with 2 hdc, 1 sc; turn.

Row 2: 1 sl st into sc, 1 sl st into hdc, 1 sc in hdc, 1 hdc in dc, 1 dc in dc until 4 sts remain on row. End with 1 hdc, 1 sc, 2 sl sts in the 4 last sts; cut yarn.

PICOT EDGING, ROUNDED:

Fold the jacket in half. The picot edging is worked through both layers up to the front opening and then only in the front to the lower edge of the opposite front. The rest of the edging is worked through both layers.

Rnd 1: With Light Pink, attach yarn with 1 sl st at the shoulder, work 1 sc in the same st as sl st, *ch 3, 1 sc in 1st ch (=1 picot), skip 3 dc*; rep from * to * to the corner. In the corner, work 1 sc, 1 picot, 1 sc in same ch; rep from * to * to next corner and then work corner as described above. Rep from * to * to the next corner; rep from * to *. Cut yarn.

TIE CORD:

Purple yarn: Crochet a chain 11¾ in / 30 cm long. Thread the cord through the picot edging, beginning at the collar (see photo).

FINISHING: Weave in all ends neatly on WS and gently steam press.

Make another potholder the same way.

Jacket Potholder, Large

MEASUREMENTS:	Approx. 7½ x 6¾ in / 19 x 17 cm
MATERIALS:	CYCA #1, Garnstudio Muskat (100% cotton; 109 yd/100 m / 50 g) / Beige 61, 100 g / Purple 04, 50 g
CROCHET HOOK:	U.S. size C-2 or D-3 / 3mm
GAUGE:	23 sts in pattern = 4 in / 10 cm in diameter

Instructions:

With Beige, ch 37.

Row 1: Beg in the 4th ch from the hook, work 2 dc in next ch, ch 1, skip 1 ch, *1 dc in ch, 2 dc in next ch, ch 1, skip 1 ch*; rep from * to * across and end with 3 dc, ch 1; turn.
Row 2: Ch 3, skip 3 dc, 1 sc in ch, *ch 2, skip 3 dc, 1 sc in ch*; rep from * to * and end with ch 2, skip 3 dc, 1 sc in 3rd ch from previous row; turn.
Row 3: Ch 3 (= 1 dc), 2 dc around ch-2 loop, ch 1, skip 1 ch, *3 dc around ch-2 loop, ch 1, skip 1 ch*; rep from * to * across, ending with 3 dc around ch-3 loop; turn.
Rows 4, 6, 8, 10, 12, 14, 16, 18, 20, 22, 24: Work as for Row 2.
Rows 5, 7, 9, 11, 13, 15, 17, 19, 21, 23: Work as for Row 3.

RIGHT FRONT:

Row 25: Work as for Row 2, but crochet only over 5 dc groups; turn.
Row 26: Work as for Row 3, but crochet only over 5 dc groups; turn.
Rows 27, 29, 31, 33, 35, 37, 39, 41, 43, 45, 47: Work as for Row 25.
Rows 28, 30, 32, 34, 36, 38, 40, 42, 44, 46, 48: Work as for Row 26.
Cut yarn.

LEFT FRONT:

Beg on Row 25, skipping over 2 dc groups (= neck); attach yarn with 1 sl st into ch.
Row 26: Work as for Row 3, but crochet only over 5 dc groups; turn.
Rows 27, 29, 31, 33, 35, 37, 39, 41, 43, 45, 47: Work as for Row 25.
Rows 28, 30, 32, 34, 36, 38, 40, 42, 44, 46, 48: Work as for Row 26.
Cut yarn.

EDGING WORKED IN THE ROUND:

With Purple, attach yarn at lower edge of back in the 1st ch of foundation chain.

Rnd 1: *Ch 2, skip 3 dc, 1 sc in ch*; rep from * to * to the corner; long side: *ch 2, skip 1 dc row, 1 sc around sc*; rep from * to * to next corner, 1 sc in 3rd ch*; continue along lower edge of front as for back to the next corner and end side with 1 sc in the 3rd dc. Next side: work as for long side and neck, 1 sc in ch, ch 2, skip 3 dc, 1 sc in ch; continue on next side as for previous side to the next corner. Crochet lower edge of front as for other front and then continue on next long side. End with 1 sl st into ch (see photo).

COLLAR:

Row 1: Count four 3-dc groups down from the shoulder and attach Purple with 1 sl st into ch, 1 sc in ch, 2 hdc in dc, 1 dc in ch, 3 dc in dc. Continue up to and including 3 dc groups past the next shoulder and end with 2 hdc, 1 sc; turn.
Row 2: 1 sl st into sc, 1 sl st into hdc, 1 sc in hdc, 1 hdc in dc, 1 dc in dc until 4 sts remain on row. End with 1 hdc, 1 sc, 2 sl sts in the 4 last sts; cut yarn.

PICOT EDGING, ROUNDED:

Fold the jacket in half. The picot edging is worked through both layers up to the front opening and then only in the front to the lower edge of the opposite front. The rest of the edging is worked through both layers.
Rnd 1: With Beige, attach yarn with 1 sl st at the shoulder, work 1 sc in the same st as sl st, *ch 3, 1 sc in 1st ch (=1 picot), skip 3 dc*; rep from * to * to the corner. In the corner, work 1 sc, 1 picot, 1 sc in same ch; rep from * to * to next corner and then work corner as described above. Rep from * to * to the next corner; rep from * to *. Cut yarn.

TIE CORD:

With Purple: Crochet a chain 13¾ in / 35 cm long. Thread the cord through the picot edging, beginning at the collar (see photo).

FINISHING: Weave in all ends neatly on WS and gently steam press.

Make another potholder the same way.

Traditional

Vintage Potholders from the 1940's

These vintage potholders were featured in a supplement to *Women and Clothing no. 7,* 1940.

The potholders are not as large as the ones we use today. I'm not sure what that signifies but it could be due to yarn shortages or maybe that was just the standard size at the time.

Crochet patterns were more basic in the 1940's. The original patterns below are followed by new versions.

Old-fashioned Striped Potholder

MEASUREMENTS:	Approx. 5½ x 5½ in / 14 x 14 cm
MATERIALS:	Original potholders, both pairs / CYCA #2, Rowan Pima cotton DK (100% cotton; 142 yd/130 m / 50 g) / Millet (Gray) 058, 50 g / Lozenge (Old Rose) 055, 50 g
CROCHET HOOK:	U.S. size G-6 / 4 mm
GAUGE:	23 sc = 4 in / 10 cm

Instructions:
With Gray, ch 5.

Row 1: Beg in the 2nd ch from hook, work 1 sc in each of next 2 ch, (1 sc, ch 1, 1 sc) in next ch, 1 sc in each of next 2 ch; turn.

Row 2: Ch 1, work 1 sc through back loop in each of next 3 sc, (1 sc, ch 1, 1 sc) around ch loop, 1 sc in back loop in each of next 3 sc; turn.

Row 3: Ch 1, work 1 sc through back loop in each of next 4 sc, (1 sc, ch 1, 1 sc) around ch loop, 1 sc in back loop in each of next 4 sc; turn.

Row 4: Ch 1, work 1 sc through back loop in each of next 5 sc, (1 sc, ch 1, 1 sc) around ch loop, 1 sc in back loop in each of next 5 sc; turn.

Row 5: Work as for Row 4, *at the same time,* increasing with 1 sc on each side of the center ch loop of row.

Rows 6 – 13: Work as for Row 4 (= 15 sc on each side of center ch).

Row 14: Change to Old Rose and work as for Row 4.

Row 15: Work as for Row 4.

Row 16: Change to Gray and work as for Row 4.

Row 17: Work as for Row 4.

Row 18: Change to Old Rose and work as for Row 4.

Row 19: Work as for Row 4; cut yarn.

Row 20: Change to Gray and work as for Row 4.

Rows 21 – 25: Work as for Row 4; cut yarn.

EDGING:

With Old Rose, attach yarn with 1 sl st at top right of chain foundation, work 1 sc in the same st, ch 10 (= hanging loop), 1 sc in the opposite side of the ch foundation. Continue directly to side 1.

Side 1: 1 sc, *ch 3, 1 sc in 1st ch (= picot), skip 1 row, 1 sc in next row*; rep from * to * along the entire side.

Sides 2-3: *Ch 3, 1 sc in 1st ch (= picot), skip 2 sc, 1 sc in next sc*; rep from * to * along the two sides.

Side 4: *Ch 3, 1 sc in 1st ch (= picot), skip 1 row, 1 sc in next row*; rep from * to * all along last side. End with 1 sl st into sc and then work 12 sc around 10-ch loop (= hanging loop); end with 1 sl st. Cut yarn.

FINISHING: Weave in all ends neatly on WS and lightly steam press potholder on back.

Make another potholder the same way.

Old-fashioned Checked Potholder

MEASUREMENTS:	Approx. 5½ x 5½ in / 14 x 14 cm
MATERIALS:	Original potholders, both pairs / CYCA #2, Rowan Pima cotton DK (100% cotton; 142 yd/130 m / 50 g) / Millet (Gray) 058, 50 g / Lozenge (Old Rose) 055, 50 g
CROCHET HOOK:	U.S. size G-6 / 4 mm
GAUGE:	23 sc = 4 in / 10 cm

Instructions:

With Old Rose, ch 31.

Row 1: Beg in 2nd ch from hook, *work 1 sc in each of next 5 ch; change to Gray and work 1 sc in each of next 5 ch*; rep from * to * across = 30 sc; turn.

Row 2: Ch 1, *with Gray, work 1 sc in each of next 5 sc; change to Old Rose and work 1 sc in each of next 5 sc*; rep from * to * across = 30 sc; turn.

Row 3: Ch 1, *with Old Rose, work 1 sc in each of next 5 sc; change to Gray and work 1 sc in each of next 5 sc*; rep from * to * across = 30 sc; turn.

Rows 4 – 5: Work as for Row 2:

Row 6: Work as for Row 3.

Row 7: Work as Row 2.

Rows 8 – 9: Work as for Row 3.

Rep Rows 2 – 9: 3 times total and then work Rows 2 – 4 once more or until potholder is square. Cut yarn.

EDGING:

Rnd 1: With Old Rose,

Side 1: Work 1 sc in each row along the side, work 3 sc in corner.

Side 2: Work 1 sc in each ch of foundation and 3 sc in corner.

Side 3: Work as for 1st side with 3 sc in corner.

Side 4: Work 1 sc in each sc across, ending with 1 sl st into 1st sc. Cut yarn.

HANGING LOOP:

Attach Old Rose with 1 sl st at the top between the Old Rose and Gray blocks (corner), 1 sc, ch 10, 1 sc in the space between the Old Rose and Gray blocks (corner) on the opposite side of the corner; turn and work 12 sc around ch loop; fasten off.

FINISHING: Weave in all ends neatly on WS and lightly steam press potholder on back.

Make another potholder the same way.

New Checked and Striped Potholders

MEASUREMENTS:	Approx. 8 x 8 in / 20 x 20 cm
MATERIALS:	New potholders, both pairs / CYCA #2, Rowan Pima cotton DK (100% cotton; 142 yd/130 m / 50 g) / Millet (Gray) 058, 50 g / Skipper (blue) 062, 50 g
CROCHET HOOK:	U.S. size G-6 / 4 mm
GAUGE:	23 sc = 4 in / 10 cm

New checked potholder

With Blue, ch 41.

Row 1: Beg in 2nd ch from hook, *work 1 sc in each of next 5 ch; change to White and work 1 sc in each of next 5 ch*; rep from * to * across = 40 sc; turn.

Row 2: Ch 1, *with White, work 1 sc in each of next 5 sc; change to Blue and work 1 sc in each of next 5 sc*; rep from * to * across = 40 sc; turn.

Row 3: Ch 1, *with Blue, work 1 sc in each of next 5 sc; change to White and work 1 sc in each of next 5 sc*; rep from * to * across = 40 sc; turn.

Row 4: Work as for Row 2.

Row 5: Work as for Row 3.

Row 6: Work as for Row 3.

Row 7: Work as Row 2.

Row 8: Work as for Row 3.

Row 9: Work as for Row 2.

Row 10: Work as for Row 3.

Row 11: Work as for Row 2.

Rep Rows 2 – 11: 4 times total or until potholder is square. Cut yarn.

EDGING:

Rnd 1: Work around with Blue as follows:

Side 1: Work 1 sc in each row along the side, work 3 sc in corner.

Side 2: Work 1 sc in each ch of foundation and 3 sc in corner.

Side 3: Work as for 1st side with 3 sc in corner.

Side 4: Work 1 sc in each sc across, ending with 1 sl st into 1st sc. Cut yarn.

HANGING LOOP:

Attach Blue with 1 sl st at the top between the Blue and White blocks (corner), 1 sc, ch 12, 1 sc in the space between the Blue and White blocks (corner) on the opposite side of the corner; turn and work 14 sc around ch loop; fasten off.

FINISHING: Weave in all ends neatly on WS and lightly steam press potholder on back.

Make another potholder the same way.

New striped potholder

With White, ch 5.

Row 1: Beg in the 2nd ch from hook, work 1 sc in each of next 2 ch, (1 sc, ch 1, 1 sc) in next ch, 1 sc in each of next 2 ch; turn.

Row 2: Ch 1, work 1 sc through back loop in each of next 3 sc, (1 sc, ch 1, 1 sc) around ch loop, 1 sc in back loop in each of next 3 sc; turn.

Row 3: Ch 1, work 1 sc through back loop in each of next 4 sc, (1 sc, ch 1, 1 sc) around ch loop, 1 sc in back loop in each of next 4 sc; turn.

Row 4: Ch 1, work 1 sc through back loop in each of next 5 sc, (1 sc, ch 1, 1 sc) around ch loop, 1 sc in back loop in each of next 5 sc; turn.

Row 5: Work as for Row 4, *at the same time*, increasing with 1 sc on each side of the center ch loop of row.

Rows 6 – 20: Work as for Row 4 (= 22 sc on each side of center ch).

Row 21: Change to Blue and work as for Row 4.

Row 22: Work as for Row 4.

Row 23: Change to White and work as for Row 4.

Row 24: Work as for Row 4.

Row 25: Change to Blue and work as for Row 4.

Row 26: Work as for Row 4.

Row 27: Change to White and work as for Row 4.

Rows 28: Work as for Row 4.

Row 29: Change to Blue and work as for Row 4.

Row 30: Work as for Row 4; cut yarn.

Row 31: Change to White and work as for Row 4.

Rows 32 – 37: Work as for Row 4; cut yarn.

EDGING:

With Blue, attach yarn with 1 sl st at top right of chain foundation, work 1 sc in the same st, ch 12 (= hanging loop), 1 sc in the opposite side of the ch foundation. Continue directly to the 1st side:

Side 1: 1 sc, *ch 3, 1 sc in 1st ch (= picot), skip 1 row, 1 sc in next row*; rep from * to * along the entire side.

Sides 2 and 3: *Ch 3, 1 sc in 1st ch (= picot), skip 2 sc, 1 sc in next sc*; rep from * to * along sides 2 and 3.

Side 4: *Ch 3, 1 sc in 1st ch (= picot), skip 1 row, 1 sc in next row*; rep from * to * all along last side. End with 1 sl st into sc and then work 14 sc around 12-ch loop (= hanging loop); end with 1 sl st. Cut yarn.

FINISHING: Weave in all ends neatly on WS and lightly steam press potholder on back.

Make another potholder the same way.

Placemat with Undulating Pattern

Measurements: Approx. 12³/₄ x 16¹/₄ in / 32.5 x 41 cm
Materials: CYCA #1, Garnstudio Muskat (100% cotton; 109 yd/100 m / 50 g) / Beige 23, 50 g / Navy Blue 13, 100 g / Petrol 74, 100 g

Note: if you want to make 4 placemats, you need 50 g each Navy Blue and Petrol for each of the three other mats
Crochet hook: U. S. E-4 / 3.5 mm and U.S. D-3 / 3.25 mm for the edging
Gauge: 18 sts in pattern with larger hook = 4 in / 10 cm

Instructions:

With larger hook and Petrol, ch 89.

Row 1: Work 2 dc in the 2ⁿᵈ ch from hook, skip 2 ch, * 1 sc, 2 dc in next ch, skip 2 ch*; rep from * to * across and end with 1 sc in the last ch; turn.

Row 2: Ch 1, 2 dc in 1 sc, skip 2 dc, *1 sc, 2 dc in next sc, skip 2 dc*; rep from * to * and end with 1 sc in ch 1 from previous row; turn.

Row 3: Work as for Row 2.

Row 4: Work as for Row 2.

Row 5: Work as for Row 2.

Row 6: Change to Navy Blue and work as for Row 2.

Rows 7 – 9: Work as for Row 2.

Row 10: Change to Beige and work as for Row 2.

Rows 11 – 13: Work as for Row 2.

Row 14: Change to Petrol and work as for Row 2.

Rows 15 – 17: Work as for Row 2.

Row 18: Change to Navy Blue and work as for Row 2.

Rows 19 – 21: Work as for Row 2.

Row 22: Change to Beige and work as for Row 2.

Rows 23 – 25: Work as for Row 2.

Row 26: Change to Navy Blue and work as for Row 2.

Rows 27 – 29: Work as for Row 2.

Row 30: Change to Petrol and work as for Row 2.

Rows 31 – 33: Work as for Row 2.

Row 34: Change to Beige and work as for Row 2.

Rows 35 – 37: Work as for Row 2.

Row 38: Change to Navy Blue and work as for Row 2.

Rows 39 – 41: Work as for Row 2.

Row 42: Change to Petrol and work as for Row 2.

Rows 43 – 46: Work as for Row 2; cut yarn.

EDGING:

Rnd 1: Change to smaller hook and Navy Blue, attaching yarn in one corner. Work ch 1, 2 sc in corner.

Side 1 (top of placemat): 1 sc in each sc and 1 sc in each ch across; work 3 sc in next corner.

Side 2 (side of the placemat): 1 sc in approx. every row; 3 sc in next corner.

Side 3 (bottom of placemat): 1 sc in every ch (foundation chain); 3 sc in next corner.

Side 4: Work as for 2ⁿᵈ side, ending with 1 sl st into 1ˢᵗ ch.

Rnd 2: Work in crab st (sc worked from left to right) all around, ending with 1 sl st into 1ˢᵗ crab st. Cut yarn.

FINISHING: Weave in all ends neatly on WS and gently steam press mat(s).

Interwoven Potholder

MEASUREMENTS:	Approx. 8 x 8 in / 20 x 20 cm
MATERIALS:	CYCA #2, Garnstudio, Cotton/Linen (53% cotton/47% linen; 93 yd/85 m / 50 g) / Black 16, 100 g / Brown 05, 100 g
CROCHET HOOK:	U.S. size C-2 or D-3 / 3 mm + U.S. size E-4 / 3.5 mm for foundation chain
GAUGE:	19 dc with smaller hook = 4 in / 10 cm

Instructions:

For each strip, with larger hook, ch 38.

Row 1: Change to smaller hook and work 1 dc in the 4th ch from hook, work 1 dc in each ch across = 35 dc; turn.
Row 2: Ch 3, 1 dc in each dc across = 35 dc; turn.
Row 3: Work as for Row 2.
Row 4: Work as for Row 2 = 1 complete strip.

Make 5 Brown strips and 5 Black strips. After completing all the strips, join them with Black.

Tip: Weave in all ends before you join the strips.

EDGING:

Rnd 1: Use smaller hook and Black. Take a Brown strip, lay a Black strip behind the Brown one and, with the short side of the Black strip against the long side of the Brown strip, crochet the strips together with 7 sc. Lay a new Black strip in front of the Brown strip and crochet these together with 7 sc. Continue with the 3 remaining Black strips and crochet them alternately in front of and behind the Brown strips. End with 3 sc in the corner st. Continue to crochet the strips together on the next side. Crochet the last Black strip together with the short side of the Brown strip from the previous side with 7 sc. Lay a Brown strip in front of the Black one and crochet them together with 7 sc. Continue as for the previous side and crochet all the Brown strips to the Black ones alternately in front of and behind Black strips. End with 3 sc in the corner st. Continue for the 3rd and 4th sides as for the previous sides. The joining sequence interweaves the strips lattice style (see photo). Finish the round with 1 sl st into the 1st sc.
Rnd 2: Work a round of crab st (1 crab st into each sc), working from left to right; end with 1 sl st into 1st sc.

HANGING LOOP:

Ch 16, 1 sl st into 1st ch; work 20 sc around loop and end with 1 sl st. Cut yarn and weave in ends.

FINISHING:

Weave in all ends neatly on WS and gently steam press.

Make another potholder the same way.

Fan Pattern Placemat

MEASUREMENTS:	Approx. 12³/₄ x 16¹/₂ in / 32 x 42 cm
MATERIALS:	CYCA #1, Garnstudio Muskat (100% cotton; 109 yd/100 m / 50 g) / Light Beige 61, 150 g / Navy Blue 13, 50 g
CROCHET HOOK:	U. S. E-4 / 3.5 mm and U.S. D-3 / 3.25 mm for the edging
GAUGE:	23 sts in pattern with larger hook = 4 in / 10 cm

Instructions:

With larger hook and Light Beige, ch 67.

Row 1: Begin with the 4th ch from hook (= 1 dc), work 1 dc into ch, *skip 2 ch, work 5 dc in next ch, skip 2 ch, 1 dc in ch 3 times*; rep from * to * across and end with skip 2 ch, 5 dc in next ch. skip 2 ch, 1 dc in ch 2 times; turn.
Row 2: Ch 3 (= 1 dc), 1 dc in dc, *skip 2 dc, 5 dc in same dc, skip 2 dc, 1 dc in dc, 1 tr inserting hook from front to back around the dc of previous row (= front post treble, see p. 108), 1 dc in dc*; rep from * to * across, ending with skip 2 dc, 5 dc in same dc, skip 2 dc, 1 dc in dc 2 times; turn.
Row 3: Ch 3 (= 1 dc), 1 dc in dc, *skip 2 dc, 5 dc in same dc, skip 2 dc, 1 dc in dc, 1 back post tr, inserting hook from back to front and around the front post tr of previous row (= relief st), 1 dc in dc*; rep from * to * and end with skip 2 dc, 5 dc in same dc, skip 2 dc, 1 dc in dc 2 times; turn.

Row 4: Ch 3 (= 1 dc), 1 dc in dc, *skip 2 dc, 5 dc in same dc, skip 2 dc, 1 dc in dc, 1 front post tr (insert hook from front to back and around the tr from previous row, 1 dc in dc*; rep from * to* across, ending with skip 2 dc, 5 dc in same dc, skip 2 dc, 1 dc in dc 2 times; turn.
Repeat Rows 3 – 4 until piece measures 15¹/₂ in / 39 cm. Cut yarn.

EDGING:

Rnd 1: With Navy Blue, attach yarn to a corner with 1 sl st. Ch 3 (= 1 dc), 6 dc in corner st, *skip 2 sts or 2 rows, 1 sc in st, skip 2 sts or 2 rows, 7 dc in same st; rep from * to * around. End with 1 sl st to top of ch 3.

FINISHING: Weave in all ends neatly on WS. Gently stream press on WS, lightly stretching mat to finished dimensions.

Chevron Placemat

MEASUREMENTS:	Approx. 12¼ x 16½ in / 31 x 42 cm
MATERIALS:	CYCA #1, Garnstudio Muskat (100% cotton; 109 yd/100 m / 50 g) / Beige 23, 100 g / Petrol 74, 50 g
CROCHET HOOK:	U. S. C-2 / 3 mm and U.S. D-3 / 3.25 mm for the edging
GAUGE:	20 sts in pattern with smaller hook = 4 in / 10 cm
PATTERN REPEAT:	14 sts

Instructions:

With smaller hook and Beige, ch 73.

Row 1: Beginning in 4th ch from hook (= 1 dc), work 1 dc in each of the next 5 ch, * skip 2 ch, 1 dc in each of the next 6 ch, ch 1, 1 dc in each of the next 6 ch*; rep from * to * and end with skip 2 ch, 1 dc in each of the last 6 ch.

Row 2: Ch 3 (= 1 dc), 2 dc in next dc, 1 dc in each of the next 3 dc, *skip 2 dc, 1 dc in each of the next 5 dc, 1 dc around ch loop, ch 1, 1 dc around same ch loop, 1 dc in each of the next 5 dc*; rep from * to *, skip 2 dc, and end with 1 dc in each of the next 3 dc, 2 dc in dc, 1 dc in 3rd ch; turn.

Row 3: Change to Petrol and work as for Row 2.

Row 4: Work as for Row 2.

Row 5: Change to Beige and work as for Row 2.

Row 6: Change to Petrol and work as for Row 2.

Row 7: Change to Beige and work as for Row 2.

Rows 8 – 33: Work as for Row 2.

Row 34: Change to Petrol and work as for Row 2.

Row 35: Change to Beige and work as for Row 2.

Row 36: Change to Petrol and work as for Row 2.

Row 37: Work as for Row 2.

Row 38: Change to Beige and work as for Row 2.

Row 39: Work as for Row 2. Cut yarn.

EDGING:

Rnd 1: With Beige and larger hook, attach yarn with 1 sl st in a corner st on foundation row. Work 1 sc in each ch along the foundation row, continue with 2 sc in the corner, 2 sc in each row along long side, 2 sc in corner, 1 sc in each st on short side, 2 sc in corner and 2 sc in each row along other long side; end with 1 sl st to 1st sc.

FINISHING: Weave in all ends neatly on WS. Gently steam press on WS, lightly stretching mat to finished dimensions.

Patchwork Placemat

MEASUREMENTS:	Approx. 13 x 17 in / 33 x 43 cm
MATERIALS:	CYCA #2, Garnstudio, Cotton/Linen (53% cotton/47% linen; 93 yd/85 m / 50 g) / Light gray 15, 100 g / Gray-blue 20, 100 g
TUNISIAN CROCHET HOOK:	U.S. size H-8 / 5.5 mm
CROCHET HOOK:	U.S. size 7 / 4.5 mm for foundation chain, last row and edging
GAUGE:	19 vertical sts with Tunisian hook U.S. H-8 / 5 mm = 4 in / 10 cm
PATTERN REPEAT:	2 vertical sts, 1 extended loop st = 3 sts

Instructions:

With crochet hook U.S. size 7 / 4.5 mm and Gray-blue, ch 76.

Row 1, forward: Change to Tunisian hook U.S. H-8 / 5 mm and pick up 76 vertical sts in the top loop of each chain in foundation = 76 loops on hook.

Row 1, return: Bind off across.

Row 2, forward: Pick up 76 vertical sts = 76 loops on hook.

Row 2, return: Bind off across.

Row 3, forward: Work as for Row 2, forward.

Row 3, return: Work as for Row 2, return.

Row 4, forward: Work as for Row 2, forward.

Row 4, return: Work as for Row 2, return.

Rows 5 – 8, forward and return: Work as for Row 2, forward and return.

Row 9, forward: With Gray-blue, pick up 1 edge st and 9 vertical sts change to Light gray (see page 109 for how to change colors in the middle of a row) and pick up 58 vertical sts, change to Gray-blue (use a separate ball of yarn), pick up 9 vertical sts and then 1 edge st.

Row 9, return: Work as for Row 2, return.

Row 10, forward: With Gray-blue, pick up 1 edge st and 9 vertical sts change to Light gray and pick up sts in pattern as follows: *2 vertical sts, 2 elongated loops (= insert hook through the piece under the return row, catching the yarn on the right side of st, repeat on the left side of the vertical st—see the explanation of elongated sts on page 113)*; rep from * to * 9 times total and end with 2 vertical sts, skip 1 vertical st, pick up 1 vertical st, yo, skip 1 vertical st, pick up 2 vertical sts, work 29 knit sts (see page 114); change to Gray-blue (use a separate ball of yarn), and then pick up 9 vertical sts and 1 edge st.

Row 10, return: Work as for Row 2, but work the elongated sts as follows: The 2 elongated sts are bound off together by pulling the yarn through 3 loops at the same time (see page 113 for working elongated sts).

Row 11, forward: With Gray-blue, pick up 1 edge st, 9 vertical sts; change to Light gray and pick up sts in pattern as follows: *2 vertical sts, 2 elongated loops (= insert hook through the piece under the return row, catching the yarn on the right side of st, repeat on the left side of the vertical st—see the explanation of elongated sts on page 113)*; rep from * to * 9 times total and end with 2 vertical sts, skip 1 vertical st, pick up 1 vertical st, yo, skip 1 vertical st, pick up 2 vertical sts, work 29 knit sts (see page 114); change to Gray-blue (use a separate ball of yarn), and then pick up 9 vertical sts and 1 edge st.

Row 11, return: Work as for Row 9, return.

Rows 12 – 13, forward and return: Work as for Row 11, forward and return.

Row 14, forward: With Gray-blue, pick up 1 edge st, 9 vertical sts; change to Light gray and pick up sts in pattern as follows: *2 vertical sts, 2 elongated loops (= insert hook through the piece under the return row, catching the yarn on the right side of st, repeat on the left side of the vertical st—see the explanation of elongated sts on page 113)*; rep from * to * 9 times total and end with 2 vertical sts, skip 1 vertical st, pick up 1 vertical st, yo, skip 1 vertical st, pick up 2 vertical sts, work 29 vertical sts; change to Gray-blue (use a separate ball of yarn), and then pick up 9 vertical sts and 1 edge st.

Row 14, return: Work as for Row 9, return.

Rows 15 – 17, forward and return: Work as for Row 14, forward and return.

Rows 18 – 21, forward and return: Work as for Row 11, forward and return.

Rows 22 – 26, forward and return: Work as for Row 14, forward and return.

Row 27, forward: Reverse the placement of the pattern blocks. With Gray-blue, pick up 1 edge st. 9 vertical sts; change to Light gray and pick up sts in pattern as follows: Pick up 1 st in each of the elongated sts (insert hook through both loops) = 29 vertical sts total and then continue to the next block: *pick up 2 vertical sts, work 2 elongated sts*; rep from * to * 9 times total and end with 2 vertical sts; change to Gray-blue and pick up 9 vertical sts and 1 edge st.

Row 27, return: Work as for Row 10, return.

Row 28, forward: With Gray-blue, pick up 1 edge st. 9 vertical sts; change to Light gray and pick up 29 knit sts total; continue to next block: *pick up 2 vertical sts, 2 elongated

sts*; rep from * to * 9 times total and end with 2 vertical sts; change to Gray-blue and pick up 9 vertical sts and 1 edge st.

Row 28, return: Work as for Row 10, return.

Rows 29 – 30, forward and return: Work as for Row 28, forward and return.

Row 31, forward: With Gray-blue, pick up 1 edge st, 9 vertical sts; change to Light gray and pick up 29 vertical sts, *2 vertical sts, 2 elongated loops *; rep from * to * 9 times total and end with 2 vertical sts; change to Gray-blue and pick up 9 vertical sts and 1 edge st.

Row 31, return: Work as for Row 10, return.

Rows 32 – 35, forward and return: Work as for Row 31, forward and return.

Rows 36 – 38, forward and return: Work as for Row 28, forward and return.

Rows 40 – 44, forward and return: Work as for Row 31, forward and return.

Row 45, forward: Continue with Gray-blue only and work as for Row 2, forward and return.

Note: Pick up 1 st in each elongated st (inserting hook through both loops).

Row 45, return: Work as for Row 10, return.

Rows 46 – 52, forward and return: Work as for Row 2, forward and return.

End with a row of slip st across using crochet hook U.S. 7 / 4.5 mm.

EDGING:

Rnd 1: With Gray-blue and crochet hook U.S. 7 / 4.5 mm, attach yarn with 1 sl st at a corner, work 1 sl st in each st of the last row; on the short sides, work 1 sl st into each edge st and work 1 sl st into each ch of foundation chain; end with 1 sl st into 1st sl st.

FINISHING: Weave in all ends neatly on WS and steam press lightly, gently stretching mat to finished dimensions.

Lace Placemat

MEASUREMENTS:	Approx. 12³/₄ x 15³/₄ in / 32 x 40 cm
MATERIALS:	CYCA #2, Garnstudio, Cotton/Linen (53% cotton/47% linen; 93 yd/85 m / 50 g) / Light gray 15, 100 g / Natural 02, 100 g
TUNISIAN CROCHET HOOK:	U.S. size H-8 / 5 mm
CROCHET HOOK:	U.S. size 7 / 4.5 mm for the foundation chain, last row and edging
GAUGE:	19 vertical sts with Tunisian hook U.S. H-8 / 5 mm = 4 in / 10 cm
PATTERN REPEAT:	7 sts in lace pattern

Instructions:

With crochet hook U.S. 7 / 4.5 mm and Light gray, ch 76.

Row 1, forward: Change to Tunisian hook U.S. H-8 / 5 mm and pick up 76 vertical sts in the top loop of each chain in foundation = 76 loops on hook.

Row 1, return: Bind off across.

Row 2, forward: Pick up 76 vertical sts = 76 loops on hook.

Row 2, return: Bind off across.

Row 3, forward: Work as for Row 2, forward.

Row 3, return: Work as for Row 2, return.

Row 4, forward: Work as for Row 2, forward.

Row 4, return: Work as for Row 2, return.

Rows 5 – 8, forward and return: Work as for Row 2, forward and return.

Row 9, forward: With Light gray, pick up 1 edge st and 9 vertical sts change to Natural (see page 109 for how to change colors in the middle of a row) and pick up sts in pattern as follows: 2 vertical sts, *yo, skip 1 vertical st, 1 vertical st, yo, skip 1 vertical st, 4 vertical sts*; rep from * to * 8 times total and end with yo, skip 1 vertical st, pick up 1 vertical st, yo, skip 1 vertical st, pick up 2 vertical sts; change to Light gray (use a separate ball of yarn), pick up 9 vertical sts and then 1 edge st. (See small inset photo above for details of pattern.)

Row 9, return: Work as for Row 2 (bind off the yarnover as for a regular st – see page 113 for how to work lace in Tunisian crochet).

Rows 10 – 44, forward and return: Work as for Row 9, forward and return.

Rows 45 – 53, forward and return: Continue with Light gray only and work as for Row 2, forward and return. End with a row of slip sts using crochet hook U.S. 7 / 4.5 mm.

EDGING:

Rnd 1: With light gray and crochet hook U.S. 7 / 4.5 mm, attach yarn with 1 sl st at a corner, work 1 sl st in each st of the last row; on the short sides, work 1 sl st into each edge st and work 1 sl st into each ch of foundation chain; end with 1 sl st into 1ˢᵗ sl st.

FINISHING: Weave in all ends neatly on WS and steam press lightly, gently stretching placemat to finished dimensions.

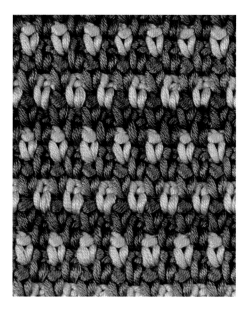

Double Potholder

MEASUREMENTS:	Approx. 8 x 8 in / 20 x 20 cm
MATERIALS:	CYCA #1, Garnstudio Muskat (100% cotton; 109 yd/100 m / 50 g) / Medium Gray 24, 100 g / Old Rose 09, 100 g / Light Gray 19, 100 g
CROCHET HOOK:	U.S. C-2 or D-3 / 3 mm
GAUGE:	26 sts in pattern = 4 in / 10 cm

Instructions:

With Medium gray, ch 50.

Row 1: With Medium Gray, work 1 sc in the 2nd ch from hook, *ch 1, skip 1 ch, 1 sc in ch*; rep from * to * across; turn.

Row 2: With Medium Gray, ch 1, 1 sc in sc, *1 sc in ch, ch 1, skip 1 sc*; rep from * to *, ending row with 1 sc in ch, 1 sc in sc; turn.

Row 3: Change to Light Gray; ch 1, 1 sc in sc, *ch 1, skip 1 sc, 1 sc in ch*; rep from * to *, ending row with ch 1, 1 sc in sc; turn.

Row 4: Change to Old Rose and work as for Row 2.

Row 5: With Old Rose, work as for Row 3.

Row 6: Change to Light Gray and work as for Row 2.

Repeat Rows 1 – 6 8 times total, ending with 2 rows Medium Gray (or until potholder is square). Make another piece the same way.

EDGING:

Place the two pieces together, with WS facing WS and join by crocheting together through both layers as follows:

Rnd 1: Attach Medium Gray to a corner, ch 1 and work 2 sc in corner.

Side 1 (top of potholder): *1 sc in sc, 1 sc in ch*; rep from * to * across and then work 3 sc in next corner.

Side 2 (side of potholder): Work 1 sc in approx. every row and then 3 sc in next corner.

Side 3 (lower edge of potholder): Work 1 sc in each ch (foundation ch) and then 3 sc in corner.

Side 4: Work as for Side 2, ending with 1 sl st into 1st ch.

Rnd 2: Ch 1, work crab st in each sc around and end with 1 sl st into first crab st. Continue directly to the hanging loop: Ch 15, attach ch with 1 sl st in corner, work 20 sc back around ch loop; cut yarn.

FINISHING: Weave in all ends neatly on WS. Gently steam press on WS.

Make another potholder the same way.

Tunisian crochet potholder

MEASUREMENTS:	8¼ x 8¼ in / 21 x 21 cm
MATERIALS:	CYCA #2, Rowan Pima cotton DK (100% cotton; 142 yd/130 m / 50 g) / Skipper blue 062, 100 g / Dijon 071, 100 g
TUNISIAN CROCHET HOOK:	U.S. size H-8 / 5 mm
CROCHET HOOK:	U.S. size G-6 / 4 mm for foundation chain and last row
GAUGE:	21 sts in pattern with Tunisian crochet hook = 4 in / 10 cm

Instructions:

FRONT:

With crochet hook U.S. size G-6 / 4 mm and Dijon, ch 40.

Row 1, forward: Change to Tunisian hook U.S. H-8 / 5 mm and work 40 vertical sts in the top loop of each ch in foundation = 40 loops on hook.

Row 1, return: Bind off across.

Row 2, forward: Pick up 40 vertical sts = 40 loops on hook.

Row 2, return: Change to Skipper and bind off across (see page 112 for how to change colors on the left side).

Row 3, forward: Work as for Row 2, forward.

Row 3, return: Change to Dijon and work as for Row 2, return.

Row 4, forward: Work as for Row 2, forward.

Row 4, return: Work as for Row 2, return.

Row 5, forward: Work as for Row 2, forward.

Row 5, return: Change to Skipper and work as for Row 2, return.

Row 6, forward: Work as for Row 2, forward.

Row 6, return: Change to Dijon and work as for Row 2, return.

Repeat Rows 4 – 6, forward and return until there are 11 stripe repeats. End with 1 forward and return row with Dijon or when the potholder is square. Bind off with slip stitch across using crochet hook U.S. size G-6 / 4 mm.

BACK:

With crochet hook U.S. size G-6 / 4 mm and Skipper, ch 40.

Row 1, forward: Change to Tunisian hook U.S. H-8 / 5 mm and work 40 vertical sts in the top loop of each ch in foundation = 40 loops on hook.

Row 1, return: Bind off across.

Row 2, forward: Pick up 40 vertical sts = 40 loops on hook.

Row 2, return: Change to Skipper and bind off across.

Row 3, forward: Work as for Row 2, forward.

Row 3, return: Change to Dijon and work as for Row 2, return.

Row 4, forward: Work as for Row 2, forward.

Row 4, return: Change to Skipper and work as for Row 2, return.

Row 5, forward: Work as for Row 2, forward.

Row 5, return: Change to Dijon and work as for Row 2, return.

Row 6, forward: Work as for Row 2, forward.

Row 6, return: Change to Skipper and work as for Row 2, return.

Repeat Rows 5 – 6, forward and return until there are 17 stripe repeats. End with 1 forward and return row with Dijon or when the potholder is square. Bind off with slip stitch across using crochet hook U.S. size G-6 / 4 mm.

Place the pieces with WS facing WS and crochet them together with sc through both layers. Using Skipper and crochet hook U.S. G-6 / 4 mm, work as follows:

Rnd 1: Attach yarn with a sl st to corner, work 3 sc in corner, 1 sc in each sl st of last row, 3 sc in next corner, 1 sc through both edge sts on side, 3 sc in next corner, 1 sc in each ch along foundation chain, 3 sc in corner, 1 sc through both edge sts on next side; end with 1 sl st to 1st sc.

Rnd 2: Ch 1, and then work 1 crab st in each st around; end with 1 sl st st to 1st crab st. Continue directly to the hanging loop: Ch 15, attach ch with 1 sl st to corner, work 20 sc around ch loop. Cut yarn.

FINISHING: Weave in all ends and stream press lightly.

Make another potholder the same way.

Tunisian Crochet Potholder with Stripes in Various Widths

MEASUREMENTS:	8¼ x 8¼ in / 21 x 21 cm
MATERIALS:	CYCA #2, Rowan Pima cotton DK (100% cotton; 142 yd/130 m / 50 g) / Skipper blue 062, 100 g / Dijon 071, 100 g
TUNISIAN CROCHET HOOK:	U.S. size H-8 / 5 mm
CROCHET HOOK:	U.S. size G-6 / 4 mm for foundation chain and last row
GAUGE:	21 sts in pattern with Tunisian crochet hook = 4 in / 10 cm

Instructions:

FRONT:
With crochet hook U.S. size G-6 / 4 mm and Skipper, ch 40.
Row 1, forward: Change to Tunisian hook U.S. H-8 / 5 mm and work 40 vertical sts in the top loop of each ch in foundation = 40 loops on hook.
Row 1, return: Bind off across.
Row 2, forward: Pick up 40 vertical sts = 40 loops on hook.
Row 2, return: Bind off across.
Row 3, forward: Work as for Row 2, forward.
Row 3, return: Work as for Row 2, return.
Row 4, forward: Change to Dijon and work as for Row 2, forward (see page 111 for how to change colors on the right side).
Row 4, return: Work as for Row 2, return.
Row 5, forward: Work as for Row 2, forward.
Row 5, return: Work as for Row 2, return.
Row 6, forward: Change to Skipper and work as for Row 2, forward.
Row 6, return: Work as for Row 2, return.
Row 7, forward: Work as for Row 2, forward.
Row 7, return: Work as for Row 2, return.
Row 8, forward: Work as for Row 2, forward.
Row 8, return: Work as for Row 2, return.
Row 9, forward: Change to Dijon and work as for Row 2, forward.
Row 9, return: Work as for Row 2, return.
Row 10, forward: Work as for Row 2, forward.
Row 10, return: Work as for Row 2, return.
Repeat Rows 6, forward and return – 10, forward and return 4 times and end with Rows 6 forward and return – 8, forward and return or until potholder is square. Bind off with slip stitch across using crochet hook U.S. size G-6 / 4 mm.

BACK:
With crochet hook U.S. size G-6 / 4 mm and Dijon, ch 40.
Row 1, forward: Change to Tunisian hook U.S. H-8 / 5 mm and work 40 vertical sts in the top loop of each ch in foundation = 40 loops on hook.
Row 1, return: Bind off across.

Row 2, forward: Pick up 40 vertical sts = 40 loops on hook.
Row 2, return: Bind off across.
Row 3, forward: Work as for Row 2, forward.
Row 3, return: Work as for Row 2, return.
Row 4, forward: Change to Skipper and work as for Row 2, forward.
Row 4, return: Work as for Row 2, return.
Row 5, forward: Work as for Row 2, forward.
Row 5, return: Work as for Row 2, return.
Row 6, forward: Change to Dijon and work as for Row 2, forward.
Row 6, return: Work as for Row 2, return.
Row 7, forward: Work as for Row 2, forward.
Row 7, return: Work as for Row 2, return.
Row 8, forward: Work as for Row 2, forward.
Row 8, return: Work as for Row 2, return.
Row 9, forward: Change to Skipper and work as for Row 2, forward.
Row 9, return: Work as for Row 2, return.
Row 10, forward: Work as for Row 2, forward.
Row 10, return: Work as for Row 2, return.
Repeat Rows 6, forward and return – 10, forward and return 4 times and end with Rows 6 forward and return – 8, forward and return or until potholder is square. Bind off with slip stitch across using crochet hook U.S. size G-6 / 4 mm.

Place the pieces with WS facing WS and crochet them together with sc through both layers. Using Skipper and crochet hook U.S. G-6 / 4 mm, work as follows:
Rnd 1: Attach yarn with a sl st to corner, work 3 sc in corner, 1 sc in each sl st of last row, 3 sc in next corner, 1 sc through both edge sts on side, 3 sc in next corner, 1 sc in each ch along foundation chain, 3 sc in corner, 1 sc through both edge sts on next side; end with 1 sl st to 1st sc.
Rnd 2: Ch 1, and then work 1 crab st in each st around; end with 1 sl st st to 1st crab st. Continue directly to the hanging loop: Ch 15, attach ch with 1 sl st to corner, work 20 sc around ch loop. Cut yarn.

FINISHING: Weave in all ends and steam press lightly.

Make another potholder the same way.

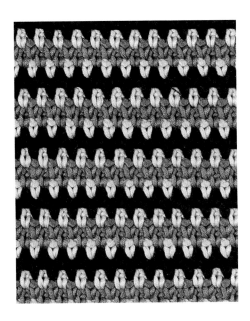

Black and Blue Striped Potholder

MEASUREMENTS:	Approx. 8 x 8 in / 20 x 20 cm
MATERIALS:	CYCA #1, Garnstudio, Muskat (100% cotton; 109 yd/100 m / 50 g) / Black 17, 50 g / Denim Blue 36, 50 g / Light Gray 19, 50 g
CROCHET HOOK:	U.S. C-2 or D-3 / 3 mm
GAUGE:	26 sts in pattern = 4 in / 10 cm

Instructions:

With black, ch 50.

Row 1, with Black: 1 sc in 2nd ch from hook, *ch 1, skip 1 ch, 1 sc in next ch*; rep from * to * across; turn.
Row 2, with Black: Ch 1, 1 sc in sc, *1 sc in ch, ch 1, skip 1 sc*; rep from * to * and end with 1 sc in ch, 1 sc in sc; turn.
Row 3, with Light Gray: Ch 1, 1 sc in sc, *ch 1, skip 1 sc, 1 sc in ch*; rep from * to * and end with ch 1, 1 sc in sc; turn.
Row 4, with Denim Blue: Work as for Row 2.
Row 5, with Denim Blue: Work as for Row 3.
Row 6, with Light Gray: Work as for Row 2.
Repeat Rows 1-6 a total of 8 times and end with 2 rows black (or end when potholder is square).

EDGING:

Rnd 1, with Denim Blue: Begin in one corner with ch 1 and 2 sc in the corner st.

Side 1 (top of the potholder): *1 sc in sc, 1 sc in ch*; rep from * to * across and then work 3 sc in the next corner st.
Side 2 (side of potholder): Work 1 sc into about every row and then 3 sc in next corner st.
Side 3 (bottom of potholder): 1 sc in each st of foundation chain.
Side 4: Work as for Side 2 and end the round with 1 sl st into 1st ch.
Rnd 2: Ch 1, work 1 crab stitch in each sc around and end with 1 sl st into 1st crab st. Continue with the hanging loop: Ch 15, join chain with 1 sl st into corner; work 20 sc around chain loop. Cut yarn.

FINISHING: Weave in all ends neatly on WS and steam press lightly.

Make another potholder the same way.

Classic Placemat

MEASUREMENTS:	Approx. 13 x 17 in / 33 x 43 cm
MATERIALS:	CYCA #2, Garnstudio, Cotton/Linen (53% cotton/47% linen; 93 yd/85 m / 50 g) / Gray-blue 20, 100 g / Dark blue 21, 150 g
TUNISIAN CROCHET HOOK:	U. S. size H-8 / 5 mm
CROCHET HOOK:	U.S. size G-6 / 4 mm for the foundation chain and last row; U.S. size 7 / 4.5 mm for edging
GAUGE:	21 sts in pattern with Tunisian hook U.S. H-8 / 5 mm = 4 in / 10 cm

Instructions:

With crochet hook U.S. size G-6 / 4 mm and Dark blue, ch 83.

Row 1, forward: Change to Tunisian hook U.S. H-8 / 5 mm and work 83 vertical sts in the top loop of each ch in foundation = 83 loops on hook.
Row 1, return: Bind off across.
Row 2, forward: Pick up 83 vertical sts = 83 loops on hook.
Row 2, return: Bind off across.
Row 3, forward: Change to Gray-blue and work as for Row 2, forward (see page 111 for how to change colors on the right side).
Row 3, return: Work as for Row 2, return.
Row 4, forward: Work as for Row 2, forward.
Row 4, return: Work as for Row 2, return.
Row 5, forward: Work as for Row 2, forward.
Row 5, return: Work as for Row 2, return.
Row 6, forward: Change to Dark Blue and work as for Row 2, forward.
Row 6, return: Work as for Row 2, return.
Row 7, forward: Change to Gray-blue and work as for Row 2, forward.
Row 7, return: Work as for Row 2, return.
Row 8, forward: Work as for Row 2, return.
Row 8, return: Work as for Row 2, return.
Row 9, forward: Change to Dark Blue and work as for Row 2, forward.
Row 9, return: Work as for Row 2, return.
Row 10, forward: Work as for Row 2, forward.

Row 10, return: Work as for Row 2, return.
Row 11, forward: Change to Dark blue and work as for Row 2, forward.
Continue, throughout, working forward and return passes as for Row 2, forward and return, changing colors in the following sequence:
Row 52, forward: Change to Gray-blue.
Row 53, forward: Change to Dark blue.
Row 54, forward: Change to Gray-Blue.
Row 56, forward: Change to Dark Blue.
Row 57, forward: Change to Gray-Blue.
Row 60, forward: Change to Dark Blue.
Row 61, forward and return: Work with Dark Blue.
With crochet hook U.S. size G-6 / 4 mm, work across in slip st to "bind off."

EDGING:

Rnd 1: Using larger crochet hook, attach Gray-blue with sl st to corner. Work 3 sc in corner, 1 sc in each sl st of last row, 3 sc in next corner, 1 sc through both loops in each st on side, 3 sc in next corner, 1 sc in each ch along foundation chain, 3 sc in corner, 1 sc through both loops in each st on next side; end with 1 sl st to 1st sc.
Rnd 2: Ch 1, and then work 1 sc in each sc around with 3 sc into each corner st; end round with 1 sl st into 1st chain.
Rnd 3: Ch 1, Work 1 sl st in each sc around and end with 1 sl st st to 1st sl st.

FINISHING: Weave in all ends neatly on WS and stream press lightly, gently stretching mat to finished dimensions.

Placemat with narrow stripes

MEASUREMENTS:	Approx. 13 x 17 in / 33 x 43 cm
MATERIALS:	CYCA #2, Garnstudio, Cotton/Linen (53% cotton/47% linen; 93 yd/85 m / 50 g) / Gray-blue 20, 100 g / Dark blue 21, 150 g
TUNISIAN CROCHET HOOK:	U. S. size H-8 / 5 mm
CROCHET HOOK:	U.S. size G-6 / 4 mm for the foundation chain and last row; U.S. size 7 / 4.5 mm for edging
GAUGE:	21 sts in pattern with Tunisian hook U.S. H-8 / 5 mm = 4 in / 10 cm

Instructions:

With crochet hook U.S. size G-6 / 4 mm and Dark blue, ch 83.

Row 1, forward: Change to Tunisian hook U.S. H-8 / 5 mm and work 83 vertical sts in the top loop of each ch in foundation = 83 loops on hook.
Row 1, return: Bind off across.
Row 2, forward: Pick up 83 vertical sts = 83 loops on hook.
Row 2, return: Bind off across.
Row 3, forward: Work as for Row 2, forward.
Row 3, return: Work as for Row 2, return.
Row 4, forward: Work as for Row 2, forward.
Row 4, return: Work as for Row 2, return.
Row 5, forward: Work as for Row 2, forward.
Row 5, return: Work as for Row 2, return.
Row 6, forward: Work as for Row 2, forward.
Row 6, return: Work as for Row 2, return.
Row 7, forward: Work as for Row 2, forward.
Row 7, return: Work as for Row 2, return.
Row 8, forward: Work as for Row 2, forward.
Continue, throughout, working forward and return passes as for Row 2, forward and return, changing colors in the following sequence:
Row 12, forward: Change to Gray-blue (see page 111 for how to change colors on the right side).
Row 13, forward: Change to Dark blue.
Row 14, forward: Change to Gray-Blue.
Row 15, forward: Change to Dark Blue.
Row 25, forward: Change to Gray-Blue.
Row 26, forward: Change to Dark Blue.
Row 27, forward: Change to Gray-Blue.
Row 28, forward: Change to Dark Blue.
Row 29, forward: Change to Gray-Blue.
Row 30, forward: Change to Dark Blue.
Row 31, forward: Change to Gray-Blue.
Row 32, forward: Change to Dark Blue.
Row 33, forward: Change to Gray-Blue.
Row 34, forward: Change to Dark Blue.
Row 35, forward: Change to Gray-Blue.
Row 36, forward: Change to Dark Blue.
Row 46, forward: Change to Gray-Blue.
Row 47, forward: Change to Dark Blue.
Row 48, forward: Change to Gray-Blue.
Row 49, forward: Change to Dark Blue.
Rows 50 – 59, forward and return: Dark-Blue.
"Bind off" with crochet hook U.S. size G-6 / 4 mm, working across in slip st.

EDGING:

Rnd 1: Using larger crochet hook, attach Dark blue with sl st to corner. Work 3 sc in corner, 1 sc in each sl st of last row, 3 sc in next corner, 1 sc through both loops in each st on side, 3 sc in next corner, 1 sc in each ch along foundation chain, 3 sc in corner, 1 sc through both loops in each st on next side; end with 1 sl st to 1st sc.
Rnd 2: Change to Gray-blue and ch 1, and then work 1 sc in each sc around with 3 sc into each corner st; end round with 1 sl st into 1st chain.
Rnd 3: Ch 1, Work 1 sl st in each sc around and end with 1 sl st st to 1st sl st.

FINISHING: Weave in all ends neatly on WS and steam press lightly, gently stretching mat to finished dimensions.

Modern

Colorful Hand Towel

Measurements:	12³/₄ x 17 in / 32 x 43.5 cm
Materials:	CYCA #1, PT Petunia (100% cotton; 120 yd/110 m / 50 g) / Lime 216, 200 g / Turquoise 274, 50 g
Crochet hook:	U.S. size G-6 / 4 mm and U.S. size F-5 / 3.75 mm for edging
Gauge:	19 sts in pattern with larger hook = 4 in / 10 cm

Instructions:

With larger hook and Lime, ch 60.

Row 1: Beginning in 4th ch from hook, work 1 dc in each ch across = 57 dc; turn.

Row 2: Ch 2, *1 front post dc around each of next 4 dc of previous row, 1 back post dc around each of next 4 dc of previous row*; rep from * to * across, ending with 1 hdc in 2nd ch; turn. (See page 108 for how to work front and back post double crochet.)

Row 3: Work as for Row 2.

Row 4: Work as for Row 2.

Row 5: Ch 2, *1 back post dc around each of next 4 dc of previous row, 1 front post dc around each of next 4 dc of previous row*; rep from * to * across, ending with 1 hdc in 2nd ch; turn.

Row 6: Work as for Row 5.

Row 7: Work as for Row 5.

Repeat Rows 2 – 7 9 times and then work Rows 2 – 4 once or until piece measures approx. 16½ in / 42 cm. Cut yarn.

EDGING:
With Turquoise and larger hook, work as follows:

Rnd 1:
Side 1: *1 sc in 2nd dc, ch 2, skip 2 dc*; rep from * to * across, ending 1 st from corner; ch 7, skip corner and 1st st on next side.

Side 2: *1 sc, ch 2, skip 2 sts*; rep from * to * evenly spaced down long side so that the edge doesn't pucker or ruffle.

Sides 3 – 4: Work as for Sides 1 – 2 ending with 1 sl st into 1st sc.

Rnd 2: Change to smaller hook, ch 1, 1 sc in sc, *2 sc around ch-2 loop, 1 sc in sc*; rep from * to * along side; work 8 sc around ch-7 loop at corner; rep from * to * along next side. Work 8 sc around ch-7 corner loop. Work the last 2 sides as for the first two sides; end rnd with 1 sl st to 1st sc.

Rnd 3: Work 1 sl st in each sc around, ending with 1 sl st to 1st sl st.

FINISHING: Weave in all ends neatly on WS and steam press lightly.

Lime and Turquoise Tunisian Crochet Potholder

MEASUREMENTS:	8 x 8 in / 20 x 20 cm
MATERIALS:	CYCA #1, PT Petunia (100% cotton; 120 yd/110 m / 50 g) / Turquoise 274, 50 g / Light Turquoise 264, 50 g / Lime 216, 100 g
TUNISIAN CROCHET HOOK:	U.S. size H-8 / 5 mm
CROCHET HOOK:	U.S. size G-6 and 7 / 4 and 4.5 mm for foundation chain and last row
GAUGE:	21 sts in pattern with Tunisian crochet hook U.S. H-8 / 5 mm = 4 in / 10 cm

Instructions:

FRONT:

With crochet hook U.S. size G-6 / 4 mm and Turquoise, ch 38.

Row 1, forward: Change to Tunisian hook U.S. H-8 / 5 mm and work 38 vertical sts in the top loop of each ch in foundation = 38 loops on hook.
Row 1, return: Bind off across.

Row 2, forward: Pick up 38 vertical sts = 38 loops on hook.
Row 2, return: Bind off across.
Row 3, forward: Work as for Row 2, forward.
Row 3, return: Work as for Row 2, return.
Row 4, forward: Change to Light Turquoise and work as for Row 2, forward (see page 111 for how to change colors on the right side).
Row 4, return: Work as for Row 2, return.
Row 5, forward: Change to Lime and work as for Row 2, forward.
Row 5, return: Work as for Row 2, return.
Row 6, forward: Work as for Row 2, forward.
Row 6, return: Work as for Row 2, return.
Row 7, forward: Change to Light Turquoise and work as for Row 2, forward.
Row 7, return: Work as for Row 2, return.
Row 8, forward: Change to Turquoise and work as for Row 2, forward.
Row 8, return: Work as for Row 2, return.
Row 9, forward: Work as for Row 2, forward.
Row 9, return: Work as for Row 2, return.
Row 10, forward: Work as for Row 2, forward.
Row 10, return: Work as for Row 2, return.
Row 11, forward: Change to Light Turquoise and work as for Row 2, forward.
Row 11, return: Work as for Row 2, return.
Row 12, forward: Change to Lime and work as for Row 2, forward.
Row 12, return: Work as for Row 2, return.
Row 13, forward: Work as for Row 2, forward.
Row 13, return: Work as for Row 2, return.
Row 14, forward: Work as for Row 2, forward.
Row 14, return: Work as for Row 2, return.
Row 15, forward: Change to Light Turquoise and work as for Row 2, forward.
Row 15, return: Work as for Row 2, return.
Row 16, forward: Change to Turquoise and work as for Row 2, forward.
Row 16, return: Work as for Row 2, return.
Row 17, forward: Work as for Row 2, forward.
Row 17, return: Work as for Row 2, return.
Row 18, forward: Work as for Row 2, forward.
Row 18, return: Work as for Row 2, return.
Row 19, forward: Change to Light Turquoise and work as for Row 2, forward.
Row 19, return: Work as for Row 2, return.
Row 20, forward: Change to Lime and work as for Row 2, forward.
Row 20, return: Work as for Row 2, return.
Row 21, forward: Work as for Row 2, forward.
Row 21, return: Work as for Row 2, return.
Row 22, forward: Work as for Row 2, forward.
Row 22, return: Work as for Row 2, return.
Row 23, forward: Change to Light Turquoise and work as for Row 2, forward.
Row 23, return: Work as for Row 2, return.

Rows 24, forward and return – 33, forward and return: Repeat from Rows 1 – 10 forward and return or until potholder is square. Finish with a row of sl st using crochet hook U.S. G-6 / 4 mm.

BACK:
With crochet hook U.S. size 7 / 4.5 mm and Turquoise, ch 38.
Row 1, forward: Change to Tunisian hook U.S. H-8 / 5 mm and work 38 vertical sts in the top loop of each ch in foundation = 38 loops on hook.
Row 1, return: Bind off.
Row 2, forward: 38 vertical sts = 38 loops on hook.
Row 2, return: Change to Light Turquoise, bind off all sts (see how to change colors on the left side on page 112).
Row 3, forward: Work as for Row 2, forward.
Row 3, return: Change to Lime and work as for Row 2, return.
Row 4, forward: Work as for Row 2, forward.
Row 4, return: Change to Turquoise and work as for Row 2, return.
Row 5, forward: Work as for Row 2, forward.
Row 5, return: Work as for Row 2 return.
Row 6, forward: Work as for Row 2, forward.
Row 6, return: Change to Light Turquoise and work as for Row 2 return.
Row 7, forward: Work as for Row 2, forward.
Row 7, return: Change to Lime and work as for Row 2 return.
Row 8, forward: Change to Turquoise and work as for Row 2, forward.
Repeat Rows 4, return – 8, forward 6 times (= 31 forward and return rows)
Row 31, return: Change to Turquoise and work as for Row 2.
Row 32, forward: Work as for Row 2, forward.
Row 32, return: Work as for Row 2, return.
Row 33, forward: Work as for Row 2, forward.
Row 33, return: Work as for Row 2, return.
Finish with 1 row sl st using hook U.S. G-6 / 4 mm.

EDGING:
Place the pieces with WS facing WS and crochet them together with sc through both layers. Using Lime and crochet hook U.S. G-6 / 4 mm, work as follows:
Rnd 1: Attach yarn with a sl st to corner, work 3 sc in corner, 1 sc in each sl st of last row, 3 sc in next corner, 1 sc through both edge sts on side, 3 sc in next corner, 1 sc in each ch along foundation chain, 3 sc in corner, 1 sc through both edge sts on next side; end with 1 sl st to 1st sc.
Rnd 2: Ch 1, *1 sc in sc, ch 2, 1 sc in 1st ch (= 1 picot), skip 1 sc*; rep from * to * around. Continue directly to the hanging loop: Ch 15, attach ch with 1 sl st to corner, work 20 sc around ch loop. Cut yarn.

FINISHING: Weave in all ends and steam press lightly.

Make another potholder the same way.

Potholder in Back and Front Post Double Crochet

MEASUREMENTS:	7³/₄ x 7³/₄ in / 19.5 x 19.5 cm
MATERIALS:	CYCA #1, PT Petunia (100% cotton; 120 yd/110 m / 50 g) / Lime 216, 50 g / Turquoise 274, 100 g
CROCHET HOOK:	U.S. size D-3 / 3.25 mm
GAUGE:	22 sts in pattern = 4 in / 10

Instructions:

With turquoise, ch 40.

Row 1: Beg in 4th ch from hook, work 1 dc in each ch across = 37 dc; turn.

Row 2: Ch 2, *1 front post dc around each of next 4 dc of previous row, 1 back post dc around each of next 4 dc of previous row*; rep from * to * across, ending with 1 hdc in 2nd ch; turn. (See page 108 for how to work front and back post double crochet.)

Row 3: Work as for Row 2.

Row 4: Work as for Row 2.

Row 5: Ch 2, *1 back post dc around each of next 4 dc of previous row, 1 front post dc around each of next 4 dc of previous row*; rep from * to * and end with 1 hdc in 2nd ch; turn.

Row 6: Work as for Row 5.

Row 7: Work as for Row 5.

Repeat Rows 2 – 7 4 times and then work Rows 2 – 4 once or until potholder is square. Cut yarn.

EDGING:

Rnd 1: Work with Lime as follows:

Side 1: *1 sc in 2nd dc, ch 2, skip 2 dc*; rep from * to * along side, stopping 1 st from corner, ch 6, skip corner + 1 st on next side.

Side 2: *1 sc, ch 2, skip 2 sts*; rep from * to * evenly spaced along side so that the piece doesn't pucker or ruffle.

Sides 3 and 4: Work as for Sides 1 and 2 , ending rnd with 1 sl st into 1st sc.

Rnd 2: Ch 1, 1 sc in sc, *2 sc around ch-2 loop, 1 sc in sc*; rep from * to * along side. Work 7 sc around ch-6 loop at corner; rep from * to * along next side. Work 7 sc around ch-6- loop in corner; work the last 2 sides as for the first two sides, ending rnd with 1 sl st to 1st sc.

Rnd 3: Work 1 sl st in each sc around, ending with 1 sl st into 1st sl st; cut yarn.

FINISHING: Weave in all ends neatly on WS and steam press lightly.

Use one corner loop as the hanging loop.

Tunisian Crochet Placemat

MEASUREMENTS:	Approx. 13 x 17 in / 33 x 43 cm
MATERIALS:	CYCA #1 PT Petunia (100% cotton; 120 yd/110 m / 50 g) / Turquoise 274, 50 g / Light Turquoise 264, 50 g / Lime 216, 50 g
TUNISIAN CROCHET HOOK:	U.S. size J-9 / 5.5 mm
CROCHET HOOK:	U.S. 7 / 4.5 mm for foundation chain, last row, and edging
GAUGE:	19 sts in pattern with larger hook = 4 in / 10 cm

Instructions:

With crochet hook U.S. 7 / 4.5 mm and Turquoise, ch 78.

Row 1, forward: Change to Tunisian hook U.S. J-9 / 5.5 mm and work 78 vertical sts in the top loop of each ch in foundation = 78 loops on hook.
Row 1, return: "Bind off" all sts.
Row 2, forward: 78 vertical sts = 78 loops on hook.
Row 2, return: Change to Light Turquoise and bind off sts across (see page 112 for how to change colors on the left side).
Row 3, forward: Work as for Row 2, forward.
Row 3, return: Work as for Row 2, return.
Row 4, forward: Work as for Row 2, forward.
Row 4, return: Work as for Row 2, return.
Row 5, forward: Work as for Row 2, forward.
Row 5, return: Work as for Row 2, return.
Row 6, forward: Work as for Row 2, forward.
Row 6, return: Change to Light Turquoise and work as for Row 2, return.
Row 7, forward: Work as for Row 2, forward.
Row 7, return: Work as for Row 2, return.
Row 8, forward: Work as for Row 2, forward.
Row 8, return: Change to Lime and work as for Row 2, return.
Row 9, forward: Work as for Row 2, forward.
Row 9, return: Work as for Row 2, return.
Row 10, forward: Work as for Row 2, forward.
Row 10, return: Work as for Row 2, return.
Row 11, forward: Work as for Row 2, forward.
Row 11, return: Change to Light turquoise and work as for Row 2, return.
Row 12, forward: Work as for Row 2, forward.
Row 12, return: Work as for Row 2, return.

Row 13, forward: Work as for Row 2, forward.
Row 13, return: Change to Turquoise and work as for Row 2, return.
Continue throughout the remainder of the piece by repeating Row 2 forward and return passes, changing colors on the following rows:
Row 19, return: Change to Light Turquoise.
Row 21, return: Change to Lime.
Row 24, return: Change to Light Turquoise.
Row 26, return: Change to Turquoise.
Row 29, return: Change to Light Turquoise.
Row 31, return: Change to Lime.
Row 34, return: Change to Light Turquoise.
Row 36, return: Change to Turquoise.
Row 42, return: Change to Light Turquoise.
Row 44, return: Change to Lime,
Row 47, return: Change to Light Turquoise.
Row 49, return: Change to Turquoise.
Rows 50 – 54, return: Work with Turquoise.
End with 1 row sl st using crochet hook U.S. 7 / 4.5 mm

EDGING:
Rnd 1: With crochet hook, attach Lime with sl st to corner. Work 3 sc in corner, 1 sc in each sl st of last row, 3 sc in next corner, 1 sc through both loops in each st on side, 3 sc in next corner, 1 sc in each ch along foundation chain, 3 sc in corner, 1 sc through both loops in each st on next side; end with 1 sl st to 1st sc.
Rnd 2: Ch 1, *1 sc in sc, ch 2, 1 sc in 1st ch (= 1 picot), skip 1 sc*; rep from * to * around. Cut yarn.

FINISHING: Weave in all ends neatly on WS and steam press lightly.

Contrasts

Potholder

MEASUREMENTS:	Approx. 8 x 8 in / 20 x 20 cm
MATERIALS:	CYCA #2, Garnstudio, Cotton/Linen (53% cotton/47% linen; 93 yd/85 m / 50 g) / Brown 05 and Beige 03, 100 g each / Garnstudio Muskat (100% cotton; 109 yd/100 m / 50 g) / Red 12, 50 g for edging.
CROCHET HOOK:	U.S. size E-4 / 3.5 mm
GAUGE:	24 sts in pattern = 4 in / 10 cm

Instructions:

With either Beige or Brown cotton/linen, ch 47.

Row 1: Work 1 dc in 3rd ch from hook and then work 1 dc in each ch across for a total of 45 dc; turn.

Row 2: Ch 3 (= 1 dc), *1 front post dc (see page 108 for more on front post double crochet) around the 2nd dc of previous row, 1 front post dc around the next dc from previous row, 1 dc in dc, 1 dc in dc*; rep from * to * across, ending with 1 dc; turn.

Rows 3 – 25 (or until potholder is square): work as for Row 2.

EDGING:

Change to Muskat Red

Rnd 1:

Side 1: *Attach yarn and work 1 sc in 2nd dc, ch 2, skip 2 dc*; rep from * to * across, ending 1 st from corner, ch 7 (hanging loop).

Side 2: Skip 1 st, *1 sc, ch 2*; rep from * to * evenly spaced along side so that the edge doesn't pucker or ruffle.

Sides 3 and 4: Work as for sides 1 and 2, omitting ch 7 at corner, and end rnd with 1 sl st into 1st sc.

Rnd 2:

Side 1: *1 sc in 1st ch, ch 3, 1 sc in 1st ch (= picot)*; rep from * to * across, work 10 sc around the ch loop at corner.

Repeat Side 1 along remaining 3 sides and end rnd with 1 sl st to 1st sc.

FINISHING: Weave in all ends neatly on WS and steam press lightly.

Make another potholder using the opposite Cotton/Linen color for the body of the potholder.

The washcloth is crocheted with a linen singles yarn while the hand towel is worked with the yarns doubled and the potholder with four strands. This is how you can vary the thickness of the crocheted fabric without using different weights of yarn. If you make all three pieces, you'll only need one spool of each color. When working with doubled or quadrupled strands, just wind up the number of balls you need from the spool of yarn.

Dish Cloth with Edgings or Stripes

MEASUREMENTS: With Stripes: Approx. 10¾ x 10¾ in / 27 x 27 cm; With Red Edging: 11½ x 11½ in / 29 x 29 cm

MATERIALS: With Stripes: CYCA #1, Textilmakeriet, Bockens 16/2 linen (100% linen, 755 yd/690 m / 125 g) / Beige 0000, unbleached, 2 spools (250 g) / Red 517, 1 spool (125 g); With Red Edging: Tekstilmakeriet, Bockens 16/2 linen (100% linen; 755 yd/690 m / 125 g) / Beige 0000 unbleached or Dark Beige 462 and Red 1007, 1 spool of each

CROCHET HOOK: With Stripes: U.S. B-1 or C-2 / 2.5 mm and U.S. A / 2 mm for the edging; with Red Edging: U.S. A – C-2 / 2-2.5 mm (**Note:** the washcloth is crocheted loosely)

GAUGE: 32 sts in pattern with U.S. 2.5 mm hook = 4 in / 10 cm. With Red Edging: 36 sts in pattern with hook U.S. B-1 – C-2 / 2.5 mm = 4 in / 10 cm

Instructions for Washcloth with Stripes:

With hook U.S. B-1 or C-2 / 2.5 mm and a single strand of Beige, ch 86.

Row 1: Work 1 sc in the 2nd ch from hook, *ch 1, skip 1 ch, 1 sc in ch*; rep from * to * across; turn.
Row 2: Ch 1, 1 sc in sc, *1 sc in ch, ch 1, skip 1 sc*; rep from * to * across and end with 1 sc in ch, 1 sc in sc; turn.
Row 3: Ch 1, 1 sc in sc, *ch 1, skip 1 sc, 1 sc in ch*; rep from * to * across and end with ch 1, 1 sc in sc; turn.
Row 4: Work as for Row 2.
Row 5: Work as for Row 3.
Row 6: Work as for Row 2.
Row 7: Change to Red and work as for Row 3.
Row 8: Work as for Row 2.
Row 9: Change to Beige and work as for Row 3.
Row 10: Work as for Row 2.
Row 11: Change to Red and work as for Row 3.
Row 12: Work as for Row 2.
Row 13: Work as for Row 3.
Row 14: Work as for Row 2.
Row 15: Change to Beige and work as for Row 3.
Row 16: Work as for Row 2.
Row 17: Change to Red and work as for Row 3.
Row 18: Work as for Row 2.

Row 19: Change to Beige and work as for Row 3.
Row 20: Work as for Row 2:
Rows 21 – 100 (80 rows or until piece is square): Alternate Rows 3 and 2. Do not cut yarn; begin edging.

EDGING:
Rnd 1: Change to smaller hook and Beige, beginning at corner: work ch 1, 2 sc in corner.
Side 1: *1 sc in sc, 1 sc in ch*; rep from * to * to next corner; work 3 sc in corner.
Side 2: Work 1 sc in approx. every row and 3 sc in next corner.
Side 3: 1 sc in each ch (foundation chain) and 3 sc in next corner.
Side 4: Work as for Side 2, ending rnd with 1 sl st into 1st ch.
Rnd 2: Ch 1, work 1 crab st in each sc around and end with 1 sl st into 1st crab st; cut yarn.

FINISHING: Weave in all ends neatly on WS and steam press lightly.

INSTRUCTIONS FOR WASHCLOTH WITH RED EDGING:
With hook to produce gauge and a single strand of Beige ch 108.

Row 1: Begin in 4th ch from hook, and work 1 dc in each ch across = 105 dc; turn.

Row 2: Ch 3 (= 1 dc), *1 front post dc around dc of previous row (insert hook from front to back – see page 108 for more information), 1 front post dc around next dc, 1 dc in dc, 1 dc in dc*; rep from * to * across, ending with 1 dc; turn.

Rows 3 – 54 (or until piece is square): Work as for Row 2.

EDGING: Change to Red.
Rnd 1:
Side 1: *Attach yarn and work 1 sc in 2nd dc, ch 2, skip 2 dc*; rep from * to * across, ending 1 st from corner, ch 7 (hanging loop).

Side 2: Skip 1 st, *1 sc, ch 2*; rep from * to * evenly spaced along side so that the edge doesn't pucker or ruffle.
Sides 3 and 4: Work as for sides 1 and 2, omitting ch 7 at corner, and end rnd with 1 sl st into 1st sc.
Rnd 2:
Side 1: *1 sc in 1st ch, ch 3, 1 sc in 1st ch (= picot)*; rep from * to * across; work 10 sc around the ch loop at corner.
Repeat Side 1 along remaining 3 sides and end rnd with 1 sl st to 1st sc.

FINISHING: Weave in all ends neatly on WS and steam press lightly.

Linen hand towel

MEASUREMENTS:	Approx. 13 x 20½ in / 33 x 52 cm
MATERIALS:	CYCA #1, Textilmakeriet, Bockens 16/2 linen (100% linen, 755 yd/690 m / 125 g) / Beige 0000, unbleached, 2 spools (250 g) / Red 517, 1 spool (125 g)
	Note: each color is worked with 2 strands of that color held together throughout.
CROCHET HOOK:	U.S. E-4 / 3.5 mm for towel and U.S. D-3 / 3.25 mm for edging
GAUGE:	22 sts in pattern with larger hook = 4 in / 10 cm.

Instructions

With larger hook and two strands of Beige linen held together, ch 72.

Row 1: Work 1 sc in the 2nd ch from hook, *ch 1, skip 1 ch, 1 sc in ch*; rep from * to * across; turn.
Row 2: Ch 1, 1 sc in sc, *1 sc in ch, ch 1, skip 1 sc*; rep from * to * across and end with 1 sc in ch, 1 sc in sc; turn.
Row 3: Ch 1, 1 sc in sc, *ch 1, skip 1 sc, 1 sc in ch*; rep from * to * across and end with ch 1, 1 sc in sc; turn.
Row 4: Work as for Row 2.
Row 5: Work as for Row 3.
Row 6: Work as for Row 2.
Row 7: Change to Red and work as for Row 3.
Row 8: Work as for Row 2.
Row 9: Change to Beige and work as for Row 3.
Row 10: Work as for Row 2.
Row 11: Change to Red and work as for Row 3.
Row 12: Work as for Row 2.
Row 13: Change to Beige and work as for Row 3.
Row 14: Work as for Row 2.
Rows 15 – 39 (25 rows): Alternate working Rows 3 and 2.
Row 40: Work as for Row 2, but work the first 8 sts of row, then ch 7, skip 7 sts (this will be the hanging loop) and then continue in pattern.
Row 41: Work as for Row 3, working in pattern across, including over the 7 ch sts of the loop.

Rows 42 – 66 (25 rows): Alternate working Rows 2 and 3.
Row 67: Change to Red and work as for Row 3.
Row 68: Work as for Row 2.
Row 69: Change to Beige and work as for Row 3.
Row 70: Work as for Row 2.
Row 71: Change to Red and work as for Row 3.
Row 72: Work as for Row 2.
Row 73: Change to Beige and work as for Row 3.
Rows 74 – 78 (5 rows): Alternately work Rows 2 and 3.

EDGING:

Rnd 1: Change to smaller hook and Beige, attaching yarn in a corner of long side of towel. Work ch 1 and 2 sc in corner.
Side 1: *sc in sc, 1 sc in ch*; rep from * to * to next corner; work 3 sc in corner.
Side 2 (short side): Work 1 sc in approx. every row and 3 sc in next corner.
Side 3 (long side): 1 sc in each ch (foundation chain) and 3 sc in next corner.
Side 4: Work as for Side 2, ending rnd with 1 sl st into 1st ch.
Rnd 2: Ch 1, work 1 crab st in each sc around and end with 1 sl st into 1st crab st; cut yarn.

FINISHING: Weave in all ends neatly on WS and steam press lightly.

Linen Potholder

MEASUREMENTS: Approx. 8 x 8 in / 20 x 20 cm

MATERIALS: CYCA #1, Textilmakeriet, Bockens 16/2 linen (100% linen, 755 yd/690 m / 125 g) / Beige 0000, unbleached, 2 spools (250 g) / Red 517, 1 spool (125 g)
Note: each color is worked with 4 strands of that color held together throughout.

CROCHET HOOK: U.S. 7 / 4.5 mm and U.S. G-6 / 4 mm for the edging

GAUGE: 18 sts in pattern with larger hook = 4 in / 10 cm.

Instructions

With larger hook and four strands of Beige linen held together, ch 36.

Row 1: Work 1 sc in the 2nd ch from hook, *ch 1, skip 1 ch, 1 sc in ch*; rep from * to * across; turn.

Row 2: Ch 1, 1 sc in sc, *1 sc in ch, ch 1, skip 1 sc*; rep from * to * across and end with 1 sc in ch, 1 sc in sc; turn.

Row 3: Ch 1, 1 sc in sc, *ch 1, skip 1 sc, 1 sc in ch*; rep from * to * across and end with ch 1, 1 sc in sc; turn.

Row 4: Work as for Row 2.

Row 5: Change to Red and work as for Row 3.

Row 6: Work as for Row 2.

Row 7: Change to Beige and work as for Row 3.

Row 8: Work as for Row 2.

Row 9: Change to Red and work as for Row 3.

Row 10: Work as for Row 2.

Row 11: Change to Beige and work as for Row 3.

Row 12: Work as for Row 2.

Rows 13 – 28 (16 rows): Alternately work Rows 3 and 2.

Row 29: Work as for Row 3, but stop when 6 sts remain (= opening for loop); end with 1 sc; turn (the rest of the potholder is worked over these sts).

Row 30 – 35 (6 rows): Alternately work Rows 2 and 3. Do not cut yarn.

EDGING:

Rnd 1: Change to smaller hook and begin at a corner with ch 1 and 2 sc in corner. Work 1 sc in each sc and ch across and then 3 sc in corner. Work in sc across the edge to the inner corner, with 1 sc in each row, 1 sc in the inner corner. On the next edge form the inner corner, work 1 sc in each ch and sc across and then 2 sc in corner, ch 8 (= hanging loop) and attach ch loop with 1 sc in corner as follows: Remove hook from ch, insert it through the previous corner, pick up st and pull through corner; continue with 1 sc in each ch of chain loop (= 8 sc). Continue onto next side with 1 sc in each row and 3 sc in corner. Next work 1 sc in each ch of foundation ch and 3 sc in corner, 1 sc in each row of the last side; end with 1 sl st into 1st ch.

Rnd 2: Ch 1, work 1 crab st into each sc around and end with 1 sl st into 1st crab st. Cut yarn.

FINISHING: Weave in all ends neatly on WS and steam press lightly.

Make another potholder the same way.

Christmas Placemat

MEASUREMENTS:	Approx. 12³/₄ x 16 in / 32.5 x 41 cm
MATERIALS:	For 2 placemats: CYCA #1, Garnstudio, Muskat (100% cotton; 109 yd/100 m / 50 g) / Red 12, 250 g / Green 44, 50 g
CROCHET HOOK:	U.S. E-4 / 3.5 for placemat and U.S. D-3 / 3.25 mm for edging
GAUGE:	23 sts in pattern with larger hook = 4 in / 10 cm

Instructions:
With larger hook and Red, ch 88.

Row 1: Work 1 sc in 2nd ch from hook, *ch 1, skip 1 ch, 1 sc in next ch*; rep from * to * across; turn.
Row 2: Ch 1, 1 sc in sc, *1 sc in ch, ch 1, skip 1 sc*; rep from * to * across and end with 1 sc in ch, 1 sc in sc; turn.
Row 3: Ch 1, 1 sc in sc, * ch 1, skip 1 sc, 1 sc in ch*; rep from * to * across and end with ch 1, 1 sc in sc; turn.
Row 4: Work as for Row 2.
Row 5: Work as for Row 3.
Repeat Rows 2 –3 until piece measures approx. 12¹/₂ in / 31.5 cm.

EDGING:
Rnd 1, with smaller hook and Red: Beg at a corner with ch 1 and 2 sc into corner st.

Side 1 (top of placemat): 1 sc in each sc and ch st along side; 3 sc in next corner.
Side 2 (short side of placemat): 1 sc in approx. every row; 3 sc in corner st.
Side 3 (lower edge of placemat): 1 sc in each ch (foundation chain); 3 sc in corner st.
Side 4: Work as for Side 2 and end rnd with 1 sl st into 1st ch.
Rnd 2: Change to Green and ch 1, then work 1 sc in each sc around, with 3 sc in each corner st; end rnd with 1 sl st to 1st ch.
Rnd 3: Work 1 crab st in each sc around and end with 1 sl st into 1st crab st. Cut yarn.

FINISHING: Weave in all ends neatly on WS and steam press lightly.

Christmas Potholder

MEASUREMENTS:	Approx. 8 x 8 in / 20 x 20 cm
MATERIALS:	CYCA #2, PT All Year (100% cotton; 87 yd/80 m / 50 g) / Red 259, 100 g / Green 251, 50 g
CROCHET HOOK:	U.S. size G-6 / 4 mm for potholder and U.S. F-5 / 3.75 mm for edging
GAUGE:	19 sc in pattern with larger hook = 4 in / 10 cm

Instructions:

With larger hook and Red, ch 34.

Row 1: Work 1 sc in 2nd ch from hook and then work 1 sc in each ch across = 33 sts; turn.
Row 2: Ch 1, work 1 sc through back loop in each sc across = 33 sts; turn.
Rows 3 – 38: Ch 1, work 1 sc through back loop in each sc across = 33 sts; turn.

EDGING:
Rnd 1, with smaller hook and Green: Attach yarn at a corner with sl st and work 3 sc into corner st.
Side 1: 1 sc in each sc along side; 3 sc in next corner.
Side 2: 1 sc in approx. every row (make sure edge doesn't pucker or ruffle); 3 sc in corner st.

Side 3: 1 sc in each ch (foundation chain); 3 sc in corner st.
Side 4: Work as for Side 2 and end rnd with 1 sl st into 1st ch.
Rnd 2: Work 1 sl st in each sc around, making a hanging loop on the last corner: end 1 sc before the corner st, ch 10, skip corner (= 3 sc) + 1 sc, attach loop with 1 sl st into next sl st. Cut yarn.

FINISHING: Weave in all ends neatly on WS and steam press lightly.

Make another potholder the same way.

Life Preserver Placemat

MEASUREMENTS:	Approx. 15½ in / 39 cm diameter
MATERIALS:	For 1 placemat: CYCA #2, Rowan Handknit Cotton (100% cotton; 92 yd/84 m / 50 g / White 263, 100 g / Red 215, 50 g / Navy 277, 50 g
	For 2 placemats: Rowan Handknit Cotton (100% cotton; 92 yd/84 m / 50 g / White 263, 150 g / Red 215, 100 g / Navy 277, 100 g
	Note: You will need a little more than 50 g White for each placemat so an extra ball of White will be enough for 8 placemats.
CROCHET HOOK:	U.S. size G-6 / 4 mm
GAUGE:	8 rnds = 4 in / 10 cm in diameter

Instructions:

With Navy, ch 4 and join into a ring with 1 sl st.

Rnd 1: Ch 1 and work 7 sc around ring; end with 1 sl st into 1st ch.

Rnd 2: Ch 1, 1 sc in same ch and then work 2 sc in each sc around, ending rnd with 1 sl st into 1st ch = 16 sc around.

Rnd 3: Ch 1, 1 sc in same ch, 1 sc in next sc, *2 sc in next sc, 1 sc in next sc*; rep from * to * around and end with 1 sl st into 1st ch = 24 sc.

Rnd 4: Ch 1, 1 sc in same ch, 1 sc in each of next sc, *2 sc in next sc, 1 sc in each of next 2 sc*; rep from * to * around and end with 1 sl st into 1st ch = 32 sc.

Rnd 5: Work as for Rnd 4 but with 3 sc between each increase = 40 sc.

Rnd 6: Ch 1, 1 sc in same ch, 1 sc in each sc around and end with 1 sl st into 1st ch.

Rnd 7: Work as for Rnd 4 but with 4 sc between each increase = 48 sc.

Rnd 8: Work as for Rnd 4 but with 5 sc between each increase = 56 sc.

Rnd 9: Work as for Rnd 4 but with 6 sc between each increase = 64 sc.

Rnd 10: Work as for Rnd 4 but with 7 sc between each increase = 72 sc.

Rnd 11: Work as for Rnd 4 but with 8 sc between each increase = 80 sc.

Rnd 12: Ch 1, 1 sc in same ch, 1 sc in each sc around and end with 1 sl st into 1st ch.

Rnd 13: Work as for Rnd 4 but with 9 sc between each increase = 88 sc.

Rnd 14: Work as for Rnd 4 but with 10 sc between each increase = 96 sc.

Rnd 15: Work as for Rnd 4 but with 11 sc between each increase = 104 sc.

Rnd 16: Work as for Rnd 4 but with 12 sc between each increase = 112 sc.

Rnd 17: Ch 1, 1 sc in same ch, 1 sc in each sc around and end with 1 sl st into 1st ch.

Rnd 18: Work as for Rnd 4 but with 13 sc between each increase = 120 sc.

Rnd 19: Ch 1, 1 sc in same ch, 1 sc in each sc around and end with 1 sl st into 1st ch.

Rnd 20: Work as for Rnd 4 but with 14 sc between each increase = 128 sc. Cut yarn.

Rnd 21: Change to White and ch 1, * 1 sc in each of next 32 sc; change to Red and work 1 sc in each of next 32 sc; change to White and work 1 sc in each of next 32 sc; Change to Red and work 1 sc in each of next 32 sc; end rnd with 1 sl st to 1st ch.

Note: When changing colors, catch the color not in use with each st (see photos on page 109).

Rnd 22: Change to White and ch 1, work 1 sc in each of next 31 sc, 2 sc in next sc; change to Red and work 1 sc in each of next 31 sc, 2 sc in next sc; change to White and work 1 sc in each of next 31 sc, 2 sc in next sc; change to Red and work 1 sc in each of next 31 sc, 2 sc in next sc; end with 1 sl st into 1st ch = 132 sc.

Rnd 23: Change to White and ch 1, work 1 sc in each of next 32 sc, 2 sc in next sc; change to Red and work 1 sc in each of next 32 sc, 2 sc in next sc; change to White and work 1 sc in each of next 32 sc, 2 sc in next sc; change to Red and work 1 sc in each of next 32 sc, 2 sc in next sc; end with 1 sl st into 1st ch = 136 sc.

Rnd 24: Change to White and ch 1, work 1 sc in each of next 16 sc, 2 sc in next sc, 1 sc in each of next 16 sc, 2 sc in next sc; change to Red and work 1 sc in each of next 16 sc, 2 sc in next sc, 1 sc in each of next 16 sc, 2 sc in next sc; change to White and work 1 sc in each of next 16 sc, 2 sc in next sc, 1 sc in each of next 16 sc, 2 sc in next sc; change to Red and work 1 sc in each of next 16 sc, 2 sc in next sc, 1 sc in each of next 16 sc, 2 sc in next sc; end with 1 sl st into 1st ch = 144 sc.

Rnd 25: Work as for Rnd 24 with 17 sc between increases = 152 sc.

Rnd 26: Increase 3 sc in each color section (= White, Red, White, Red) as follows: White: *1 sc in each of next 12 sc, 2 sc in next sc, 1 sc in each of next 11 sc, 2 sc in next sc, 1 sc in each of next 12 sc, 2 sc in next sc*; rep from * to * in each of the following color sections (Red, White, Red) = 164 sc.

Rnd 27: Increase 4 sc in each color section (= White, Red, White, Red) as follows: White: *1 sc in each of next 9 sc, 2 sc in next sc, 1 sc in each of next 9 sc, 2 sc in next sc, 1 sc in each of next 10 sc, 2 sc in next sc, 1 sc in each of next 9 sc, 2 sc in next sc*; rep from * to * in each of the following color sections (Red, White, Red) = 180 sc.

Rnd 28: Increase 4 sc in each color section (= White, Red, White, Red) as follows: White: *1 sc in each of next 10 sc, 2 sc in next sc, 1 sc in each of next 10 sc, 2 sc in next sc, 1 sc in each of next 11 sc, 2 sc in next sc, 1 sc in each of next 10 sc, 2 sc in next sc*; rep from * to * in each of the following color sections (Red, White, Red) = 196 sc.

Rnd 29: Increase 4 sc in each color section (= White, Red, White, Red) as follows: White: *1 sc in each of next 6 sc, 2 sc in next sc, 1 sc in each of next 11 sc, 2 sc in next sc, 1 sc in each of next 11 sc, 2 sc in next sc, 1 sc in each of next 11 sc, 2 sc in next sc, 1 sc in each of the next 6 sc*; rep from * to * in each of the following color sections (Red, White, Red) = 212 sc (= 53 sc in each color section).

Rnd 30: Increase 4 sc in each color section (= White, Red, White, Red) as follows: White: *1 sc in each of next 12 sc, 2 sc in next sc, 1 sc in each of next 12 sc, 2 sc in next sc, 1 sc in each of next 13 sc, 2 sc in next sc, 1 sc in each of next 12 sc, 2 sc in next sc*; rep from * to * in each of the following color sections (Red, White, Red) = 228 sc (57 sc in each color section).

Rnd 31: Increase 4 sc in each color section (= White, Red, White, Red) as follows: White: *1 sc in each of next 7 sc, 2 sc in next sc, 1 sc in each of next 13 sc, 2 sc in next sc, 1 sc in each of next 13 sc, 2 sc in next sc, 1 sc in each of the next 7 sc*; rep from * to * in each of the following color sections (Red, White, Red) = 244 sc (61 sc in each color section).

Rnd 32: Increase 3 sc in each color section (= White, Red, White, Red) as follows: White: Ch 1, *1 sc in each of next 19 sc, 2 sc in next sc, 1 sc in each of next 20 sc, 2 sc in next sc, 1 sc in each of next 19 sc, 2 sc in next sc*; rep from * to * in each of the following color sections (Red, White, Red) = 256 sc. End rnd with 1 sl st into 1st ch (= 64 sc in each color section).

Rnd 33: Increase 3 sc in each color section (= White, Red, White, Red) as follows: White: Ch 1, *1 sc in each of next 10 sc, 2 sc in next sc, 1 sc in each of next 21 sc, 2 sc in next sc, 1 sc in each of next 21 sc, 2 sc in next sc, 1 sc in each of next 9 sc*; rep from * to * in each of the following color sections (Red, White, Red) = 268 sc. End rnd with 1 sl st into 1st ch (= 67 sc in each color section).

Rnd 34: Increase 2 sc in each color section (= White, Red, White, Red) as follows: White: Ch 1, *1 sc in each of next 32 sc, 2 sc in next sc, 1 sc in each of next 33 sc, 2 sc in next sc;* rep from * to * in each of the following color sections (Red, White, Red) = 276 sc; end with 1 sl st into 1st ch (69 sc in each color section).

Rnd 35: Increase 1 sc in each color section (= White, Red, White, Red) as follows: White: ch 1, *1 sc in each of next 68 sc, 2 sc in next sc;* rep from * to * in each of the following color sections (Red, White, Red) = 280 sc; end with 1 sl st into 1st ch (70 sc in each color section). Cut Red yarn.

Rnd 36, with White: Ch 1, *work 1 sc in each of next 17 sc, ch 40, skip 36 sc, 1 sc in each of next 17 sc*; rep from * to * around and end with 1 sl st into 1st ch.

Rnd 37: Ch 1, *1 sl st into each of next 17 sc, 1 sc into each of next 40 ch, 1 sl st into each of next 17 sc*; rep from * to * around and end with 1 sl st into 1st ch.

FINISHING: Weave in all ends neatly on WS and steam press lightly.

Life Preserver Potholder

MEASUREMENTS:	Approx. 8 in / 20 cm diameter
MATERIALS:	CYCA #2, Rowan Handknit Cotton (100% cotton; 92 yd/84 m / 50 g / White 263, 50 g / Red 215, 50 g / Navy 277, 50 g
CROCHET HOOK:	U.S. size G-6 / 4 mm
GAUGE:	8 rnds = 4 in / 10 cm in diameter

Instructions:

With Navy, ch 4 and join into a ring with 1 sl st.

Rnd 1: Ch 1 and work 7 sc around ring; end with 1 sl st into 1st ch.

Rnd 2: Ch 1, 1 sc in same ch and then work 2 sc in each sc around, ending rnd with 1 sl st into 1st ch = 16 sc around.

Rnd 3: Ch 1, 1 sc in same ch, 1 sc in next sc, *2 sc in next sc, 1 sc in next sc*; rep from * to * around and end with 1 sl st into 1st ch = 24 sc.

Rnd 4: Ch 1, 1 sc in same ch, 1 sc in each of next 2 sc, *2 sc in next sc, 1 sc in each of next 2 sc*; rep from * to * around and end with 1 sl st into 1st ch = 32 sc.

Rnd 5: Work as for Rnd 4 but with 3 sc between each increase = 40 sc.

Rnd 6: Ch 1, 1 sc in same ch, 1 sc in each sc around and end with 1 sl st into 1st ch.

Rnd 7: Work as for Rnd 4 but with 4 sc between each increase = 48 sc.

Rnd 8: Work as for Rnd 4 but with 5 sc between each increase = 56 sc.

Rnd 9: Work as for Rnd 4 but with 6 sc between each increase = 64 sc.

Rnd 10: Change to White and ch 1, 1 sc in same ch, 1 sc in each of next 15 sc; change to Red and work 1 sc in each of next 16 sc; change to White and work 1 sc in each of next 16 sc; change to Red and work 1 sc in each of next 16 sc; end rnd with 1 sl st to 1st ch.

Note: When changing colors, catch the color not in use with each st (see photos on page 109).

Rnd 11: Change to White and ch 1, work 1 sc in each of next 7 sc, 2 sc in next sc, 1 sc in each of next 7 sc, 2 sc in next sc; change to Red and work 1 sc in each of next 7 sc, 2 sc in next sc, 1 sc in each of next 7 sc, 2 sc in next sc; change to White and work 1 sc in each of next 7 sc, 2 sc in next sc, 1 sc in each of next 7 sc, 2 sc in next sc; change to Red and work 1 sc in each of next 7 sc, 2 sc in next sc, 1 sc in each of next 7 sc, 2 sc in next sc; end with 1 sl st into 1st ch = 72 sc.

Rnd 12: Work as for Rnd 11 with 8 sc between increases = 80 sc.

Rnd 13: Work as for Rnd 11 with 9 sc between increases = 88 sc.

Rnd 14: Work as for Rnd 11 with 10 sc between increases = 96 sc.

Rnd 15: Work as for Rnd 11 with 11 sc between increases = 104 sc.

Rnd 16: Work as for Rnd 11 with 12 sc between increases = 112 sc.

Rnd 17: Work as for Rnd 11 with 13 sc between increases = 120 sc.

Rnd 18: Work as for Rnd 11 with 14 sc between increases = 128 sc.

Rnd 19: Work as for Rnd 11 with 15 sc between increases = 136 sc. Cut Red yarn.

Rnd 20, with White: Ch 1, *1 sc in each of next 8 sc, ch 23, skip 18 sc, 1 sc in each of next 8 sc*; rep from * to * and end rnd with 1 sl st into 1st ch.

Rnd 21: Ch 1, *1 sl st into each of next 8 sc, 1 sc in each of next 23 ch, 1 sl st in each of next 8 sc*; rep from * to * and end rnd with 1 sl st into 1st ch.

FINISHING: Weave in all ends neatly on WS and steam press lightly on WS.

Make another potholder the same way.

CHAIN STITCH (CH):

Step 1: Make a slip knot, insert hook into loop and bring yarn from the ball through the loop with the hook; tighten yarn to firm up the loop around the hook.

Step 2: Hold the hook in your right hand and the yarn over your left index finger. With yarn over the hook, bring hook through the loop already on hook and then you have a chain st (ch). Continue the same way until you have the desired number of stitches in the chain. Most crochet pieces begin with either a crochet foundation chain or ring.

Step 3: If you are going to work with single crochet (sc), half double crochet (hdc), double crochet (dc), or treble crochet (tr), begin by inserting the hook into the chain st indicated in the pattern. First wrap the yarn the correct number of times around the hook for the stitch (the example here is once around the hook for a double crochet) and then insert the hook into the 4th chain from the hook and complete the stitch. The first 3 chain sts count as one dc.

Step 4: With yarn around hook, pull through the loops until the stitch is completed and then work across the foundation chain in pattern (the photos shows a row of dc).

Step 5: Making a ring: Insert hook into the 1st chain (beg st) and pull yarn through both loops at the same time.

Step 6: Completed chain ring.

SINGLE CROCHET (SC) THROUGH BOTH LOOPS

Step 1: Insert hook through both loops on top of stitch, yarn around hook.

Step 2: Pull the yarn through both stitch loops.

Step 3: Yarn around hook and through both loops on the hook.

Step 4: When only one loop remains on the hook, you've completed 1 sc; repeat steps 1-3 for each single crochet.

Note: Slip stitches are made as for single crochet but, in step 2, the yarn is pulled through the stitch and the loops on the hook at the same time. Slip stitches are used to join the end to the beginning of a round. You can also use slip stitches to taper the end so it isn't visible. Slip stitch all around the edge of a piece will make the edge firmer and stronger.

SINGLE CROCHET THROUGH BACK LOOPS

Step 1: Insert hook through the back loop of stitch, yarn around hook.

Step 2: Pull the yarn through the back loop of the stitch.

Step 3: Yarn around hook and through both loops on the hook.

Step 4: When only one loop remains on the hook, you've completed 1 sc; repeat steps 1-3 for each single crochet. Working single crochet into the back loops only produces a ribbed effect and a very elastic fabric.

HALF DOUBLE CROCHET (HDC) THROUGH BOTH LOOPS

Step 1: Yarn around hook and insert hook through both loops on top of stitch, yarn around hook.

Step 2: Pull the yarn through both stitch loops.

Step 3: Yarn around hook and through all 3 loops on the hook.

Step 4: When only one loop remains on the hook, you've completed 1 hdc; repeat steps 1-3 for each half double crochet.

HALF DOUBLE CROCHET THROUGH BACK LOOPS

Step 1: Insert hook through the back loop of stitch, yarn around hook.

Step 2: Pull the yarn through the back loop of the stitch.

Step 3: Yarn around hook and through all 3 loops on the hook.

Step 4: When only one loop remains on the hook, you've completed 1 hdc; repeat steps 1-3 for each half double crochet. Working half double crochet through the back loops only produces a very elastic ribbed fabric, although single crochet through back loops makes a more elastic fabric.

DOUBLE CROCHET (DC)

Step 1: Yarn around hook and insert hook through both loops at top of stitch, yarn around hook.

Step 2: Pull the yarn through both stitch loops.

STEP 3: Yarn around hook (there are now 3 loops on hook), pull yarn through the first 2 loops on hook (2 loops now remain on hook). Yarn around hook and through both loops on hook.

STEP 4: When only one loop remains on the hook, you've completed 1 dc; repeat steps 1-3 for each double crochet.

TREBLE CROCHET (TR)

Step 1: Yarn around hook twice and insert hook through both loops at top of stitch, yarn around hook. Pull the yarn through both stitch loops.

Step 2: Yarn around hook (there are now 4 loops on the hook) and pull yarn through the first 2 loops on hook (3 loops now remain on hook).

Step 3: Yarn around hook and through two loops on hook (2 loops remain on hook). Yarn around hook; pull yarn through rem 2 loops on hook.

Step 4: When only one loop remains on the hook, you've completed 1 tr; repeat steps 1-3 for each treble crochet.

Note: A double treble (dbl tr) is worked the same way but begun with yarn around the hook 3 times; a triple treble begins with yarn around the hook 4 times.

Special Stitches

Crab stitch is single crochet worked in the opposite direction, that is, from left to right.

This stitch is used most often as a finishing or edging and is crocheted from left to right, giving the stitch an extra "twist."

Step 1: Do not turn work after the last row. After completing last row, insert hook through both loops of the first stitch to the right, turn hook so that you can pick up the yarn and bring yarn around hook.

Step 2: Pull yarn through the stitch.

Step 3: Yarn around hook and pull through both loops on hook.

Step 4: When only 1 loop remains on hook and the crab stitch has been completed, repeat Steps 1-3 for each crab stitch.

EXTENDED DOUBLE CROCHET (EDC) (SOMETIMES CALLED "LONG DOUBLE CROCHET")

Step 1: Yarn around hook and then insert hook through both loops of stitch below, yarn around hook and bring through both stitch loops.

Step 2: Yarn around hook and through only the first loop on the hook.

Step 3: Yarn around hook (there are now 3 loops on hook) and pull the new loop through the first 2 loops on hook (2 loops remain on hook). Yarn around hook and bring through remaining 2 loops on hook.

Step 4: When only 1 loop remains on hook, the extended double crochet has been completed, repeat steps 1-3 for each extended double crochet.

Edc is used for filet crochet. If you separate each edc with 2 ch, then you create a square hole.

BOBBLE

Step 1: Work one dc up to last step and leave loop on hook; work the next 3 dc the same way – all 4 dc are worked into the same stitch.

Step 2: Yarn around hook.

Step 3: Pull yarn through all loops on the hook.

Step 4: Work 1 sc into the next st to "lock" the bobble.

RELIEF STITCHES (FRONT AND BACK POST DOUBLE OR TREBLE CROCHET)

Step 1: Yarn around hook and insert hook, beg on front of work, behind the dc of previous row, and through to front.

Step 2: Yarn around hook. There should now be 1 st, 1 yarnover, 1 dc and 1 yarnover on hook.

Step 3: Bring the last yarnover through under the dc.

Step 4: Yarn around hook and complete the dc as usual.

Note: The relief st in double or treble crochet can be worked from the front as described above or from the back. When working the stitch from the back, insert the hook around the dc (or tr) in the row below beginning from the back of the row.

Two-Color Crochet

Lay the strand not being used loosely across the top of the previous row.

Work 1 sc as usual but insert the hook through the stitch of previous row and also under the unused strand so that it will stay "inside" the new single crochet.

Tug the unused strand a bit as you work from stitch to stitch.

Changing Colors in the Middle of a Row

Work up to the last yarnover around the hook with the old color and then yarnover with the new color.

Bring the new color through the loops on the hook.

Continue with the new color. Each new stitch will be formed completely with the correct color.

You can find a video about crocheting with two colors and changing colors at www.tovefevang.no.

FOUNDATION CHAIN

Step 1: Using a crochet hook one size smaller than for project, make a foundation chain.

Step 2: Change to the project hook and hold as for a knitting needle with the hook pointing down and slightly towards you in the right hand and the yarn over the left index finger. Insert the hook into the top loop of the first chain, catch the yarn and pull it through. You now have one loop/stitch – leave it on the hook.

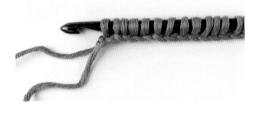

Step 3: Continue, picking up 1 loop in each chain across = one completed forward row.

Step 4: Yarn around hook and pull through the first two loops on the hook.

Step 5: Yarn around hook and pull through the next two loops on the hook.

Step 6: Continue "binding off" until all the stitches have been worked.

Step 7: A completed return row.

Every piece of Tunisian crochet begins with a chain row, picking up stitches through the chain row and a return row.

Every row has two parts: the forward row and the return row (also called the forward pass and return pass).

This is the starting point for the various stitches that you can make with Tunisian crochet.

VERTICAL STITCHES

Step 1: Insert hook through the back of the vertical stitch and yarn around hook.

Step 2: Pull the yarn through the stitch.

Step 3: Repeat Steps 1 and 2 up to the last stitch on the forward row.

Step 4: Yarn around hook, insert hook through both loops of the last stitch (= edge st) and bring through. A completed forward row.

Step 5: Yarn around hook and through the first two loops on the hook.

Step 6: Yarn around hook and through the next two loops on hook.

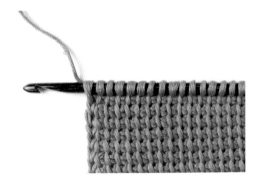

Step 7: Continue "binding off" until all the stitches have been worked = completed return row.

Step 8: Vertical stitches.

CHANGING COLORS ON THE RIGHT SIDE OF THE ROW

Step 1: A loop and the last stitch from the previous row should be on the hook.

Step 2: Change colors and bring the yarnover through the stitch.

Step 3: Work a new forward row.

Step 4: Work the return row, changing colors at the end if desired.

Step 5: Changing colors on the right side produces a "clean" stripe.

CHANGING COLORS ON THE LEFT SIDE OF THE ROW

Step 1: End the forward row before the edge st, change colors and finish the edge st as usual (the edge stitch will have the new color).

Step 2: Complete the return row.

Step 3: Work a new forward row.

Step 4: Work the return row, changing colors again.

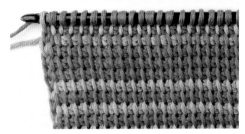

Step 5: Work a new forward row. Changing the color on the left side produces "tweedy" stripes.

Changing the color on the right and left sides each produces a different effect. No matter which side you change colors on, you will still work forward and return rows.

LACE STITCHES

Step 1: Work an edge st and then 3 vertical stitches, *yarn around hook, skip 1 st, 1 vertical st in next st*; rep from * to * across or as pattern indicates = forward row.

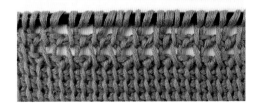

Step 2: Work the return row as usual, considering each yarnover as a regular stitch = return row.

Step 3: Work edge st and then 3 vertical stitches, *yarn around hook, skip 1 lace st, 1 vertical st in next st*; rep from * to * across or as pattern indicates = forward row.

Repeat the forward and return rows.

ELONGATED STITCHES/LOOPS

Step 1: Work edge st, 3 vertical sts, *2 vertical sts, insert hook through work under previous return row and catch the yarn on the right side; repeat on the left side of the vertical stitch = 2 elongated sts*; rep from * to * across or as pattern indicates = forward row.

Step 2: "Bind off" the vertical stitches as usual, working the two elongated stitches together (the yarn comes through 3 loops) = return row.

Repeat forward and return rows.

When binding off the elongated stitches at the end of the piece or when changing to another pattern, join the two elongated stitches together as if one stitch.

"KNIT" STITCHES

Step 1: Pick up loops by inserting hook through the vertical stitches and under the previous return row.

Step 2: Yarn around hook and through the stitch; repeat across, ending with the edge st = forward row. Work the return row as usual.
Repeat forward and return rows.

CHANGING COLORS IN THE MIDDLE OF A ROW

Step 1: With color 1, pick up the desired number of loops; change to color 2 and continue picking up loops = forward row.

Step 2: Bind off, working up to the last stitch with color 2, catch color 1 and twist the yarns around each other to avoid a hole. Bind off the rest of the stitches with color 1 = return row.

Repeated forward and return rows.

Repeated forward and return rows on the wrong side – the colors are twisted around each other at each color change.

Step 1: Change to a crochet hook one or two sizes smaller than project hook. Insert hook through the vertical stitch, yarn around hook.

Step 2: Bring the yarn through both loops on the hook at the same time.

Repeat Steps 1 and 2, working 1 sl st through each vertical stitch.

When you've completed the row, cut yarn and bring tail through last loop.

ABBREVIATIONS

beg	begin, beginning
ch	chain
dc	double crochet
	(British: treble crochet)
dtr	double treble
	(British: triple treble)
edc	extended double crochet
hdc	half double crochet
	(British: half treble crochet)
rep	repeat
rnd	round
RS	right side
sc	single crochet
	(British: double crochet)
sl st	slip stitch
st(s)	stitch(es)
tog	together
tr	treble
	(British: double treble)
WS	wrong side
yo	yarnover/yarn around hook (British: yarn over hook/yoh)

GENERAL INFORMATION

Extended dc (edc): yarn around hook, insert hook into st, yarn around hook, pull yarn through, yarn around hook, bring yarn through 1 loop on hook, *yarn around hook and bring through 2 loops on hook*; rep * to * 2 times. **Note:** Substitute ch 3 for 1 edc at beginning of row.

Dc cluster: Work the specified number of stitches (indicated before the words "dc-cluster") into the same stitch or around a chain loop; for example, 3-dc cluster.

Crab stitch = single crochet worked from left to right.

Bobble = Work 1 dc up to the last time yarn is pulled through the stitch and leave the loop on the hook. Do the same with the next three stitches which are worked into the same stitch. Yarn around hook and through all the loops on the hook at the same time. Work 1 sc in the next st (the sc stabilizes the bobble).

Front post dc = Yarn around hook and, beginning at front of work, insert hook behind the dc of previous row and out to front of work. Yarn around hook – there should now be 1 st, 1 yarnover, 1 dc and 1 yarnover on hook. Bring the last yarnover through, under the dc. Yarn around hook and complete the dc as usual. You can work either a back or a front post dc. When the dc is worked from the back, insert the hook around the dc of the previous round beginning from the back of the work.

Decreasing 1 dc = Work 1 dc but stop when there are 2 loops left on the hook. Work 1 dc into next st but stop when there are 3 loops left on the hook. Yarn around hook and bring through all 3 loops. Single crochet and half double crochet can be decreased the same way.

Increasing 1 dc = Work 2 dc into the same stitch. Single crochet and half double crochet can be increased the same way.

Check your gauge! If it is not correct, change hook size. If there are too many stitches in 4 in / 10 cm, use a larger hook; if there are too few stitches, use a smaller hook.

GARNSTUDIO DROPS available at:
Nordic Mart
San Luis Obispo, CA, US
805-542-9303
www.nordicmart.com

WEBS – AMERICA'S YARN STORE
75 Service Center Road
Northampton, MA 01060
800-367-9327
www.yarn.com
customerservice@yarn.com

VÄVSTUGA SWEDISH WEAVING & FOLK
ARTS
16 Water Street
Shelburne Falls, MA 01370
413-625-8241
www.vavstuga.com
Bockens linen, cotton and cottolin yarns

WESTMINSTER FIBERS
8 Shelter Drive
Greer, SC 29650
info@westminsterfibers.com
www.westminsterfibers.com
Rowan

WEBSITES
Many other yarn suppliers and useful
information can be found on the internet.
These are just a few websites.
www.tekstilmakeriet.no
www.garnstudio.com
www.ptdesigns.no

For more information on selecting or
substituting yarn contact your local
yarn shop or an online store, they are
familiar with all types of yarns and would
be happy to help you. Additionally, the
online knitting community at Ravelry.com
has forums where you can post ques-
tions about specific yarns. Yarns come
and go so quickly these days and there
are so many beautiful yarns available.